Transport A

CW00501911

ARRANGEMENT OF SECTIONS

A

PART V

MISCELLANEOUS AND GENERAL

Miscellaneous

General

A 2

ELIZABETH II

Transport Act 1981

1981 CHAPTER 56

An Act to make provision with respect to the disposal by the British Railways Board of part of their undertaking, property, rights and liabilities; to provide for the reconstitution of the British Transport Docks Board under the name of Associated British Ports and to confer on a company powers over that body corresponding to the powers of a holding company over a wholly-owned subsidiary; to dissolve the National Ports Council and amend the Harbours Act 1964; to make further provision for promoting road safety; to make provision with respect to road humps; to provide a new basis of vehicle excise duty for goods vehicles; to amend the law as to the payments to be made for cab licences and cab drivers' licences; to make provision for grants to assist the provision of facilities for freight haulage by inland waterway; to make provision with respect to railway fires; to amend Schedules 7 and 8 to the Public Passenger Vehicles Act 1981; and for connected purposes.   [31st July 1981]

A 3

Be it enacted by the Queen's most Excellent Majesty, by and with the advice and consent of the Lords Spiritual and Temporal, and Commons, in this present Parliament assembled, and by the authority of the same, as follows:—

Part I

Subsidiary Activities of British Railways Board

Railways
Board's
powers of
disposal.

1.—(1) Without prejudice to any powers conferred on them by any other enactment, the Railways Board shall have power to provide for the disposal, in such manner as they think fit, of—

(a) any securities of one of their subsidiaries which are held by the Board or by another of their subsidiaries ; or

(b) the whole or any part of the undertaking of, or of any property, rights or liabilities of, any of their subsidiaries.

(2) The Board shall not exercise their powers under subsection (1)(a) above except with the consent of the Secretary of State.

1968 c. 73.

(3) For the purpose of facilitating the eventual disposal under this section of any part of their undertaking or of any property, rights or liabilities the Board may exercise their powers to establish subsidiaries and to transfer property, rights and liabilities to subsidiaries under section 7 of the Transport Act 1968, notwithstanding any provision of any enactment which may be taken to limit the circumstances in which, or the purposes for which, those powers may be exercised.

(4) In exercising their powers under this section the Board may, with the consent of the Secretary of State, provide for employees' share schemes to be established in respect of any of their subsidiaries ; and any such scheme may provide for the transfer of shares without consideration.

(5) In this section "employees' share schemes" means schemes for encouraging or facilitating the holding of shares or debentures in a company by or for the benefit of—

(a) the bona fide employees or former employees of the company or of a subsidiary of the company ; or

(b) the wives, husbands, widows, widowers or children or step-children under the age of 18 of such employees or former employees.

The new
harbours
company.

2.—(1) The Railways Board shall secure that—

1948 c. 38.

(a) a company (the "harbours company") limited by shares, the objects of which include the acquisition of property, rights and liabilities in accordance with the provisions of this Part, is formed by Sealink and registered under the Companies Act 1948 before the expiry of the initial period ; and (*b*) the harbours undertaking of Sealink is transferred to the harbours company.

(2) For the purposes of this section the harbours undertaking of Sealink shall be taken to be—

(*a*) all the property, rights and liabilities comprised in that part of Sealink's undertaking which consists of the following harbours—

Folkestone, Harwich, Heysham, Holyhead, Newhaven, Parkeston Quay, Stranraer, Gravesend West Station Pier, Tilbury Floating Landing Stage, Ryde Pier, Lymington Pier, New Holland Pier, Fishbourne and Portsmouth Harbour Railway Jetty; and

(*b*) the securities of the Fishguard and Rosslare Railways and Harbours Company held by Sealink.

(3) In consideration of the transfer of property, rights and liabilities in accordance with this section the harbours company shall issue securities of the company to Sealink.

(4) Sealink shall make, and before the expiry of the initial period send to the Secretary of State, a scheme for the transfer to the harbours company of all the property, rights and liabilities which are required by this section to be so transferred.

(5) The scheme may contain such supplementary, incidental and consequential provision as may appear to Sealink to be necessary or expedient.

(6) The scheme shall not come into force unless it has been approved by the Secretary of State or until such date as the Secretary of State may, in giving his approval, specify; and the Secretary of State may approve a scheme either without modifications or with such modifications as, after consultation with Sealink, he thinks fit.

(7) On the coming into force of the scheme the property, rights and liabilities in question shall, subject to subsection (8) below, be transferred and vest in accordance with the scheme.

(8) Schedule 4 to the Transport Act 1968 (supplementary provisions as to certain transfers of property, rights and liabilities) shall apply in relation to the scheme as it applies in relation to any scheme made under section 7 of that Act.

1968 c. 73.

3.—(1) The Secretary of State may, after consultation with the Railways Board, give directions to the Board requiring them—

Power of Secretary of State to give directions.

(*a*) to exercise their powers under section 1 of this Act in a specified manner and in relation to a specified subsidiary;

(*b*) to establish a subsidiary and exercise their powers under section 7 of the Transport Act 1968 (transfer

PART I

1962 c. 46.

1974 c. 48.

Provisions
supplementary
to ss. 1 to 3.

1948 c. 38.

Associated
British Ports
and its
Holding
Company.

of property, rights and liabilities to subsidiaries) in a specified manner.

(2) It shall be the duty of the Board (notwithstanding any duty imposed on them by section 3(1) of the Transport Act 1962) to give effect to any directions given under this section.

(3) In this section " specified " means specified in directions given by the Secretary of State under this section.

(4) Any directions under this section shall be given in writing.

(5) In section 4(5) of the Railways Act 1974 (duty of Board to include certain information in the annual report made under section 4), after the words " 1962 Act ", in paragraph (*b*), there are inserted the words " section 3 of the Transport Act 1981 ".

4.—(1) Schedule 1 to this Act has effect for the purpose of making certain provisions supplementing sections 1 to 3 of this Act.

(2) In this Part of this Act—

" harbours company " has the meaning given in section 2(1)(*a*) ;

" initial period " means the period of three months beginning with the commencement of this Part ;

" Railways Board " means the British Railways Board ;

" Sealink " means Sealink U.K. Limited ;

" securities " includes shares, debentures, debenture stock, bonds and other securities of the company concerned, whether or not constituting a charge on the assets of the company ;

" subsidiary " means a subsidiary as defined in section 154 of the Companies Act 1948.

PART II

RECONSTITUTION OF BRITISH TRANSPORT DOCKS BOARD

5.—(1) As from the appointed day, the British Transport Docks Board shall be known as Associated British Ports and the following provisions of this Part have effect with respect to the constitution, powers and duties of that body.

(2) As from the appointed day, a company (referred to in this Part as " the Holding Company ") shall have the powers in relation to Associated British Ports conferred on it by the following provisions of this Part, being powers corresponding to the powers of a holding company over a wholly-owned subsidiary ; and for the purposes of any enactment Associated British Ports shall be deemed to be such a subsidiary of the Holding Company.

(3) The Secretary of State shall by order made by statutory instrument taking effect on the appointed day designate as the Holding Company a company limited by shares, formed and registered under the Companies Act 1948, in which all the issued shares are held by the Secretary of State or by nominees for him.

(4) In this Part the " appointed day " means such day as the Secretary of State may, with the consent of the Treasury, appoint for the purposes of this section by order made by statutory instrument.

6.—(1) The commencing capital debt of Associated British Ports and any liability of Associated British Ports in respect of sums borrowed from the Secretary of State are extinguished as from the appointed day.

(2) On the appointed day—

> (a) Associated British Ports shall issue to the Holding Company such securities, and pay to the Holding Company such sum of money, as the Secretary of State may direct ; and

> (b) the Holding Company shall issue to the Secretary of State or, if he so directs, to nominees for him such shares and securities of the company, and shall pay to him such sum of money, as he may direct.

(3) Shares issued in pursuance of subsection (2)(b) shall be of such nominal value and shall be deemed to have been issued for such consideration as the Secretary of State may direct.

(4) The Secretary of State may give directions as to the manner in which the various matters provided for by the preceding provisions of this section are to be dealt with in the accounts of Associated British Ports and the Holding Company for the period beginning with or including the appointed day.

(5) In ascertaining for the purposes of section 39 of the Companies Act 1980 the profits of the Holding Company which are available for distribution, any amount which by virtue of the Secretary of State's direction is to be treated as a revenue reserve of the company shall be treated as accumulated, realised profits of the company.

(6) In ascertaining for the purposes of section 56 of the Companies Act 1948 what amount falls to be treated as a premium received on the issues of shares by the Holding Company in pursuance of subsection (2)(b), the amount which in accordance with the Secretary of State's direction is to be deemed to be the consideration for the issue shall be taken to be reduced by such amount as the Secretary of State may direct to be treated as a revenue reserve of the company.

1948 c. 38.

PART II

(7) The Secretary of State shall not give any directions for the purposes of this section without the consent of the Treasury, and shares or securities of the Holding Company held by the Secretary of State or by nominees for him shall not be disposed of except with the consent of the Treasury and in such manner and on such terms as the Treasury may direct.

(8) There shall be paid into the Consolidated Fund—

(a) any sum paid to the Secretary of State by the Holding Company under subsection (2)(b);

(b) any dividends or other sums received by the Secretary of State or his nominees in right of, on the disposal of or otherwise in connection with any shares or securities of the Holding Company.

(9) Directions given by the Secretary of State under this section to Associated British Ports or the Holding Company shall be in writing.

(10) The first report prepared by the directors of the Holding Company under section 157 of the Companies Act 1948 after the appointed day shall contain a statement of every direction given by the Secretary of State under this section.

Constitution of Associated British Ports, etc.

7.—(1) Associated British Ports continues to be a body corporate.

(2) The members of Associated British Ports shall be known as directors.

(3) The number of directors of Associated British Ports shall be determined by the Holding Company from time to time, but shall not be less than five or more than thirteen.

(4) The directors of Associated British Ports shall be appointed by the Holding Company for such period as the Holding Company may determine but, without prejudice to any claim for damages for breach of contract, may be removed by the Holding Company at any time.

(5) The provisions of Schedule 2 have effect with respect to the constitution and proceedings of Associated British Ports and related matters.

Powers of Associated British Ports.

8.—(1) The provisions of Schedule 3 have effect with respect to the powers of Associated British Ports.

(2) In favour of a person dealing in good faith with Associated British Ports, any transaction decided on by the directors of Associated British Ports shall be deemed to be one which it is within the capacity of Associated British Ports to enter into

and the power of the directors shall be deemed to be free of any limitation imposed by or by virtue of any provision of this Part.

(3) A person dealing with Associated British Ports is not bound to enquire as to the capacity of Associated British Ports to enter into a transaction or as to any such limitation on the powers of the directors as is mentioned in subsection (2), and shall be presumed to have acted in good faith unless the contrary is proved.

(4) Associated British Ports shall exercise its control over its subsidiaries so as to ensure that they do not engage in activities which Associated British Ports itself has no power to engage in.

9.—(1) It is the duty of Associated British Ports to provide port facilities at its harbours to such extent as it may think expedient.

General duties of Associated British Ports.

(2) Associated British Ports shall have due regard to efficiency, economy and safety of operation as respects the services and facilities provided by it and its subsidiaries.

(3) In the performance of its functions Associated British Ports shall have regard to the interests in general of its employees and the employees of its subsidiaries.

(4) This section does not impose any form of duty or liability enforceable, either directly or indirectly, by proceedings before any court.

10.—(1) The provisions of the Companies Acts 1948 to 1980 mentioned in subsection (2) apply to Associated British Ports, subject to the adaptations specified in subsection (3), as if Associated British Ports were a public company registered in England and Wales under the Companies Act 1948 and as if the directors of Associated British Ports were the directors of such a company ; and the supplementary provisions of those Acts relating to the interpretation, operation and enforcement of those provisions apply accordingly.

Provisions of the Companies Acts applying to Associated British Ports. 1948 c. 38.

(2) The provisions referred to in subsection (1) are the following—

Subject-matter	Provisions applied
1. Financial assistance for purchase of shares, &c.	Companies Act 1948, section 54.
2. Register of charges.	Companies Act 1948, sections 104 and 105.

PART II	Subject-matter	Provisions applied
1948 c. 38.	3. Accounts and audit.	Companies Act 1948, sections 149 to 156, 158(2), 161, 163, 196, 454(1) and Schedule 8 ; Companies Act 1967, sections 3 to 8, 11, 13 and 14 (except subsections (2) and (7)) ; Companies Act 1976, sections 1 to 6, 12, 13, 18 and 19 ; Companies Act 1980, sections 54 to 56, 58 and 59.
1967 c. 81.		
1976 c. 69.		
1980 c. 22.		
	4. Directors' report.	Companies Act 1948, section 157 ; Companies Act 1967, sections 15 to 20 and 22.
	5. Disclosure by directors of interests in contracts, &c.	Companies Act 1948, section 199.
	6. Power of Court to give relief in certain cases.	Companies Act 1948, section 448.
	7. Restrictions on distributions.	Companies Act 1980, sections 39, 40 and 43.

(3) The provisions mentioned in subsection (2) apply to Associated British Ports with the following adaptations—

(a) any reference to the date of incorporation of Associated British Ports shall be construed as a reference to the appointed day ;

(b) any reference to the registered office of Associated British Ports shall be construed as a reference to its principal office ;

(c) any reference to the members of Associated British Ports shall be construed as a reference to the Holding Company and any reference to shares in Associated British Ports shall be disregarded ;

(d) documents required to be laid before Associated British Ports in general meeting shall instead be sent to the Holding Company, and any reference to documents so laid shall be construed accordingly.

(4) The Secretary of State may by regulations make such amendments of subsections (1) to (3) as appear to him necessary or expedient in consequence of changes in company law coming into force after the passing of this Act.

(5) Regulations under subsection (4) shall be made by statutory instrument which shall be subject to annulment in pursuance of a resolution of either House of Parliament.

11.—(1) The directors of Associated British Ports shall from time to time pay to the Holding Company such sums as appear to them to be justified by the profits of Associated British Ports.

(2) For the purpose of sections 39 and 40 of the Companies Act 1980 (restrictions on distributions) such payments by Associated British Ports are distributions.

(3) For the purpose of the said section 40 (restriction on extent to which distributions may reduce a company's net assets) the undistributable reserves of Associated British Ports include—

(a) any capital reserve arising from the capital debts extinguished by section 6(1) ;

(b) any reserve arising from payments made by the Holding Company on terms that the amount paid form part of Associated British Ports' undistributable reserves.

(4) In section 157(1) of the Companies Act 1948 (directors' report) as it applies to Associated British Ports the reference to the amount recommended by the directors to be paid by way of dividend shall be construed as a reference to the amount proposed by them to be paid to the Holding Company under subsection (1).

12.—(1) Associated British Ports shall keep at its principal office—

(a) a copy of any rules for the time being prescribed by the Holding Company under paragraph 4 of Schedule 2 with respect to the proceedings of the directors of Associated British Ports ;

(b) a statement of the limit for the time being set by the Holding Company under paragraph 21(5) of Schedule 3 on the aggregate amount of borrowing and guarantees by Associated British Ports and its subsidiaries ; and

(c) a statement of any restrictions for the time being imposed by the Holding Company under paragraph 22 of that Schedule on the financial arrangements which may be entered into by Associated British Ports and its subsidiaries ;

and those documents shall, during normal business hours, be made available for inspection by any person on request.

(2) It is an offence for Associated British Ports to fail to comply with a request under subsection (1).

(3) An offence under subsection (2) is punishable on summary conviction with a fine not exceeding £200.

PART II

Transfer of
functions of
Holding
Company.

13.—(1) The Holding Company may nominate another company to be Holding Company in its place and, subject to subsection (2), the provisions of this Part thenceforth have effect as if references to the Holding Company were references to the nominated company.

(2) A nomination under this section does not affect references to the Holding Company in section 6, this subsection and paragraphs 4, 7(1) and (4) and 8 of Schedule 4 ; and those references remain references to the company designated under section 5(3).

(3) A nomination under this section does not affect the validity of anything done before the nomination takes effect by or in relation to the company making the nomination, and anything which when the nomination takes effect is in process of being done by or in relation to that company may, if it relates to any functions transferred by virtue of the nomination, be continued by or in relation to the company nominated.

(4) Any appointment or rule made, limit set, restriction imposed, or other thing done by or on behalf of a company making a nomination under this section in connection with any functions transferred by virtue of the nomination shall, if in force when the nomination takes effect, have effect as if made, set, imposed or done by or on behalf of the nominated company so far as that is required for continuing its effect after the nomination takes effect.

(5) A company may not be nominated under this section unless it is controlled by the company designated under section 5(3) ; and if a company so nominated ceases to be so controlled—

    (*a*) its functions as Holding Company cease to be exercisable except for the power conferred by this section ; and

    (*b*) it shall forthwith nominate under this section the company designated under section 5(3) or a company controlled by that company.

1948 c. 38.

(6) In this section " company " means a company limited by shares which is formed and registered under the Companies Act 1948 ; and for the purposes of this section a company is controlled by another company if, and only if, all the issued voting shares in the company are held by that other company or by a company controlled by that other company.

Provisions
supplementary
to ss. 5 to 13.

14.—(1) The provisions of Part I of Schedule 4, being provisions supplementary to or consequential on the other provisions of this Part, have effect as from the appointed day.

(2) The other provisions of this Part have effect subject to the transitional provisions and savings contained in Part II of that Schedule.

(3) In this Part—　　　　　　　　　　　　　　　　　

" the appointed day " has the meaning given by section 5(4) ;

" enactment " means any provision of a public general Act, of a local, private or personal Act, of a provisional order confirmed by an Act or any regulations, order, scheme, byelaws or similar instrument made under an Act ;

" harbour " has the same meaning as in the Harbours Act 1964 ;　　　　　　　　　　　　　　　　　　1964 c. 40.

" the Holding Company ", subject to section 13(1), means the company designated by the Secretary of State under section 5(3) ;

" pension ", in relation to a person, means a pension, whether contributory or not, of any kind whatsoever payable to or in respect of him, and includes a gratuity so payable and a return of contributions to a pension fund, with or without interest thereon or any other addition thereto and any sums payable on or in respect of the death of that person ;

" pension fund " means a fund established for the purposes of paying pensions ;

" pension scheme " includes any form of arrangement for the payment of pensions, whether subsisting by virtue of an Act of Parliament, trust, contract or otherwise ;

" port facilities " means—

　　(*a*) the constructing, improving, maintaining, regulating, managing, marking or lighting of a harbour or any part thereof ;

　　(*b*) the berthing, towing, moving or dry-docking of a ship which is in, or is about to enter, or has recently left, a harbour ;

　　(*c*) the loading or unloading of goods, or embarking or disembarking of passengers, in or from any such ship ;

　　(*d*) the lighterage or the sorting, weighing, warehousing or handling of goods in a harbour ; and

　　(*e*) the movement of goods within a harbour ;

" shares " includes stock ;

" securities ", in relation to a body corporate, includes debentures, debenture stock, bonds and other securities of the body corporate, whether or not constituting a charge on the assets of that body ;

" subsidiary " means a subsidiary as defined in section 154 of the Companies Act 1948 ;　　　　　　　　　　　1948 c. 38.

" wholly-owned subsidiary " means a subsidiary all the issued shares of which are beneficially owned by the body of which it is a subsidiary, or by one or more other wholly-owned subsidiaries of that body, or partly by that body and partly by any wholly-owned subsidiary of that body.

(4) References in this Part to Associated British Ports' business or undertaking include any business or undertaking carried on by a subsidiary of Associated British Ports.

(5) References in this Part to Associated British Ports' harbours include any harbour for the time being owned or managed by Associated British Ports or by any of its subsidiaries.

PART III

DISSOLUTION OF NATIONAL PORTS COUNCIL AND AMENDMENT OF THE HARBOURS ACT 1964

Dissolution of National Ports Council.

15.—(1) On such day as the Secretary of State may appoint by order made by statutory instrument the functions of the National Ports Council shall determine, and—

(a) so much of any enactment as requires any person to consult, or do anything else in relation to, the Council, or makes consultation with, or the doing of anything else in relation to, the Council a condition precedent to the taking of any action by any person, shall cease to have effect ; and

(b) all the property, rights, liabilities and obligations which immediately before the appointed day were property, rights, liabilities and obligations of the Council shall, by virtue of this section, become property, rights, liabilities and obligations of the Secretary of State.

(2) Subsection (1) has effect subject to Part I of Schedule 5 which contains further provisions relating to the dissolution of the Council.

(3) The Secretary of State shall repay to the National Loans Fund an amount equal to the debts of the Council to the Secretary of State outstanding immediately before the appointed day.

(4) Sums received by the Secretary of State by virtue of subsection (1)(b) or by virtue of paragraph 4(2)(b) of Schedule 5 shall, if not applied in making the repayment mentioned in subsection (3), be paid into the Consolidated Fund.

(5) In this section and Part I of Schedule 5—

" the appointed day " means the day appointed by the Secretary of State under subsection (1) ;

" the Council " means the National Ports Council ;

" enactment " means any provision of a public general Act, of a local, private or personal Act, of a provisional order confirmed by an Act or any regulations, order, scheme, byelaws or similar instrument made under an Act.

16.—(1) The Secretary of State shall levy from harbour auth- orities such contributions as appear to him necessary to meet the expenses specified in subsection (2) after making allowance for the contribution made by him in accordance with subsection (3).

(2) The expenses referred to in subsection (1) are—

(*a*) the expenses of the Secretary of State in making the repayment to the National Loans Fund mentioned in section 15(3) ;

(*b*) his expenses in discharging any debts or other liabilities to which he becomes subject by virtue of section 15(1)(*b*) or paragraph 4(2)(*b*) of Schedule 5 ; and

(*c*) expenses incurred by him under paragraph 4(3) or (5), 7, 8(4)(*b*) or 9(5) of Schedule 5.

(3) The Secretary of State's contribution to those expenses is—

(*a*) all sums received by him by virtue of section 15(1)(*b*) or paragraph 4(2)(*b*) of Schedule 5, and

(*b*) a further contribution of £1.5 million, made by such instalments as he may determine with the consent of the Treasury.

(4) Sums received by the Secretary of State by virtue of this section shall be paid into the Consolidated Fund.

(5) In this section and section 17 " harbour authority " means a person engaged (whether or not in the exercise of statutory functions) in improving, maintaining or managing a harbour within the meaning of the Harbours Act 1964.

17.—(1) Contributions under section 16 shall be levied by means of one or more schemes made by the Secretary of State, referred to in this section as " charging schemes ".

(2) A charging scheme shall be made by statutory instrument which shall be subject to annulment in pursuance of a resolution of either House of Parliament.

(3) A charging scheme may apply to all harbour authorities, subject to subsection (4), to harbour authorities of a particular class or to particular harbour authorities, and may make provision for levying different contributions from different harbour authorities to whom it applies.

PART III

1964 c. 40.

(4) No contribution shall be levied from a harbour authority under a charging scheme if the only harbour being improved, maintained or managed by them is a fishery harbour or marine work within the meaning of the Harbours Act 1964.

(5) The provisions of Part II of Schedule 5 have effect with respect to charging schemes.

Amendments of the Harbours Act 1964.

18.—(1) The Harbours Act 1964 is amended in accordance with Schedule 6.

(2) With the exception of paragraph 10, the provisions of Schedule 6 come into force on the day appointed by the Secretary of State under section 15(1).

(3) Paragraph 10 of Schedule 6 comes into force on such day as the Secretary of State may appoint by order made by statutory instrument.

(4) So far as may be necessary for the purposes of any amendment by this Act of the Harbours Act 1964, references in that Act to the Minister shall be construed as references to the Secretary of State.

PART IV

ROAD SAFETY

Disqualification for repeated offences.

19.—(1) Where a person is convicted of an offence involving obligatory or discretionary disqualification and the court does not order him to be disqualified (whether on that or any other conviction) but orders particulars of the conviction to be endorsed under section 101 of the 1972 Act, the endorsement ordered shall include—

(a) particulars of the offence, including the date when it was committed ; and

(b) the number of penalty points shown in respect of the offence in Schedule 7 to this Act (or, where a range of numbers is so shown, a number falling within the range) ;

but if a person is convicted of two or more such offences the number of penalty points to be endorsed in respect of those of them that were committed on the same occasion shall be the number or highest number that would be endorsed on a conviction of one of those offences.

(2) Where a person is convicted of an offence involving obligatory or discretionary disqualification and the penalty points to be taken into account under subsection (3) number twelve or more, the court shall order him to be disqualified

for not less than the minimum period defined in subsection (4)
unless the court is satisfied, having regard to all the circumstances not excluded by subsection (6), that there are grounds
for mitigating the normal consequences of the conviction and
thinks fit to order him to be disqualified for a shorter period
or not to order him to be disqualified.

(3) The penalty points to be taken into account on the
occasion of a person's conviction are—

    (*a*) any that on that occasion will be ordered to be endorsed
        on any licence held by him or would be so ordered
        if he were not then ordered to be disqualified ; and

    (*b*) any that were on a previous occasion ordered to be
        so endorsed, unless the offender has since that
        occasion and before the conviction been disqualified,
        whether under subsection (2) or under section 93
        of the 1972 Act ;

but if any of the offences was committed more than three years
before another the penalty points in respect of that offence
shall not be added to those in respect of the other.

(4) The minimum period referred to in subsection (2) is—

    (*a*) six months if no previous disqualification imposed
        on the offender is to be taken into account ; and

    (*b*) one year if one, and two years if more than one, such
        disqualification is to be taken into account ;

and a previous disqualification imposed on an offender is to
be taken into account if it was imposed within the three years
immediately preceding the commission of the latest offence in
respect of which penalty points are taken into account under
subsection (3).

(5) Where an offender is convicted on the same occasion of
more than one offence involving obligatory or discretionary
disqualification—

    (*a*) not more than one disqualification shall be imposed on
        him under subsection (2) ; and

    (*b*) in determining the period of the disqualification the
        court shall take into account all the offences ; and

    (*c*) for the purposes of any appeal any disqualification
        imposed under subsection (2) shall be treated as an
        order made on the conviction of each of the offences.

(6) No account is to be taken under subsection (2) of—

    (*a*) any circumstances that are alleged to make the offence
        or any of the offences not a serious one ;

    (*b*) hardship, other than exceptional hardship ; or

(c) any circumstances which, within the three years immediately preceding the conviction, have been taken into
account under that subsection in ordering the offender
to be disqualified for a shorter period or not ordering
him to be disqualified.

(7) For the purposes of this section—

(a) an order for endorsement which was made before the
commencement of this section counts as an order made
in pursuance of subsection (1) for the endorsement of
3 penalty points, unless a disqualification was imposed
on the offender on that or any subsequent occasion ;
and

(b) circumstances which have been taken into account
under section 93(3) of the 1972 Act in ordering an
offender to be disqualified for a shorter period or not
ordering him to be disqualified shall be treated as
having been so taken into account under subsection
(2) of this section.

(8) The Secretary of State may by order made by statutory
instrument—

(a) alter the number of penalty points shown in Schedule
7 in respect of an offence (or, where a range of
numbers is shown, alter that range) ; and

(b) provide for different numbers to be so shown in respect
of the same offence committed in different circumstances ;

but no such order shall be made unless a draft of it has been
laid before Parliament and approved by resolution of each
House of Parliament.

(9) References in this section to disqualification do not include
a disqualification imposed under section 103 of the 1972 Act
(interim disqualification on committal to Crown Court) or section
1973 c. 62. 44 of the Powers of Criminal Courts Act 1973 (disqualification
by Crown Court where vehicle was used for commission of
offence).

Removal of **20.** Where, in pursuance of section 93(5) of the 1972 Act, a
disqualifica- period of disqualification was imposed on an offender in addition
tion. to any other period or periods then, for the purpose of determining whether an application may be made under section 95 of that
Act for the removal of either or any of the disqualifications the
periods shall be treated as one continuous period of disqualification.

21.—(1) Where—

    (*a*) in dealing with a person convicted of an endorseable offence a court was deceived regarding any circumstances that were or might have been taken into account in deciding whether or for how long to disqualify him ; and

    (*b*) the deception constituted or was due to an offence committed by that person ;

then, if he is convicted of that offence, the court by or before which he is convicted shall have the same powers and duties regarding an order for disqualification as had the court which dealt with him for the endorseable offence but shall in dealing with him take into account any order made on his conviction of the endorseable offence.

(2) In this section " endorseable offence " means an offence involving obligatory or discretionary disqualification.

22. The following subsection is inserted after subsection (3) of section 161 of the 1972 Act : —

    " (3A) Where a person has been required under section 101(4) of this Act to produce a licence to the court and fails to do so a constable may require him to produce it and, upon its being produced, may seize it and deliver it to the court." .

23.—(1) In section 88(1) of the 1972 Act the following words are inserted after paragraph (*d*) : —

    " but regulations may authorise or require the Secretary of State to refuse a provisional licence authorising the driving of a motor cycle of a prescribed class if the applicant has held such a provisional licence and the licence applied for would come into force within the prescribed period beginning at the end of the period for which the previous licence authorised (or would, if not surrendered or revoked, have authorised) the driving of such a motor cycle or beginning at such other time as may be prescribed." .

(2) In section 88 of the 1972 Act the following is substituted for paragraph (*c*) of subsection (2) (provisional licence not to authorise driving of certain motor cycles) : —

    " (*c*) shall not authorise a person, before he has passed the test of competence to drive prescribed under section 85 of this Act, to drive a motor cycle having two wheels only, unless it is a learner motor cycle as defined in subsection (2A) below or its first use (as defined in regulations) occurred before 1st January 1982 and the cylinder capacity of its engine does not exceed 125 cubic centimetres ; "

and after that subsection there are inserted the following subsections : —

"(2A) A learner motor cycle is a motor cycle which either is propelled by electric power or has the following characteristics—

(*a*) the cylinder capacity of its engine does not exceed 125 cubic centimetres ;

(*b*) the maximum power output of its engine does not exceed 9 kilowatts (as measured in accordance with International Standards Organisation standard 4106-1978.09.01) ; and

(*c*) its power to weight ratio does not exceed 100 kilowatts per metric tonne, the power being the maximum power output mentioned in paragraph (*b*) above and the weight that mentioned in subsection (2B) below.

(2B) The weight referred to in subsection (2A) above is the weight of the motor cycle with a full supply of fuel in its tank, an adequate supply of other liquids needed for its propulsion and no load other than its normal equipment, including loose tools.".

(3) In section 88(4) of the 1972 Act the following is substituted for paragraph (*b*) (full licence not to be available as provisional licence for certain motor cycles) : —

"(*b*) unless he has passed the test there mentioned, a motor cycle which, by virtue of subsection (2)(*c*) above, a provisional licence would not authorise him to drive before he had passed that test ".

(4) In subsection (1) of section 89 of the 1972 Act (duration of licences)—

(*a*) at the end of the words preceding the paragraphs there are added the words " subject to subsection (1A) below " ;

(*b*) in paragraph (*a*) for the words " (*b*) or (*c*) " there are substituted the words " or (*b*) " ;

(*c*) in paragraph (*aa*) the words " or (*c*) " are omitted and the word " and " is added at the end ; and

(*d*) paragraph (*c*) and the " and " preceding it are omitted.

(5) After subsection (1) of section 89 of the 1972 Act there is inserted the following subsection : —

"(1A) To the extent that a provisional licence authorises the driving of a motor cycle of a prescribed class it shall, unless previously surrendered or revoked, remain in force

for such period as may be prescribed or, if the licence is
granted to the holder of a previous licence which was
surrendered, revoked or treated as being revoked, for the
remainder of the period for which the previous licence
would have authorised the driving of such a motor cycle, or,
in such circumstances as may be prescribed, for a period
equal to that remainder at the time of surrender or re-
vocation.".

(6) If regulations under subsection (2) of section 85 of the
1972 Act make provision for a test of competence to drive to
consist of separate parts—

> (*a*) they may make for each part any provision that could
> be made for a test not consisting of separate parts, and
> provision for the supply by the Secretary of State of
> forms for certificates evidencing the results and for
> charges to be made for the supply ; and

> (*b*) subsection (3) of that section (appeals) shall apply in
> relation to each part as well as in relation to the whole
> of the test.

(7) In section 85(2)(*b*) of the 1972 Act (fees for driving tests)
after " such amount as may be specified in the regulations "
there is inserted " or, in such cases as may be prescribed,
specified by such person as may be prescribed ".

24.—(1) In section 193(1) of the 1972 Act and in section 103(1)   Electrically
of the Road Traffic Regulation Act 1967 (certain vehicles not to   assisted pedal
be treated as motor vehicles) the following is inserted at the end   cycles.
of paragraph (*b*): " and   1967 c. 76.

> (*c*) an electrically assisted pedal cycle of such class as may
> be prescribed by regulations so made ".

(2) An electrically assisted pedal cycle of a class specified in
regulations made for the purposes of section 193 of the 1972 Act
and section 103 of the Road Traffic Regulation Act 1967 shall
not be driven on a road by a person under the age of fourteen ;
and if any person—

> (*a*) drives such a pedal cycle ; or

> (*b*) knowing or suspecting that another person is under the
> age of fourteen, causes or permits him to drive such
> a pedal cycle ;

in contravention of this subsection he shall be guilty of an
offence.

(3) An offence under subsection (2) above shall be punishable
on summary conviction with a fine not exceeding £50.

PART IV
New
provisions
as to offences
relating
to alcohol
and drugs.

25.—(1) In section 5 of the 1972 Act (driving etc. under influence of drink or drugs) the following is added at the end of subsection (3) : —

" but in determining whether there was such a likelihood the court may disregard any injury to him and any damage to the vehicle.".

(2) The following is substituted for subsection (5) of that section : —

" (5) A constable may arrest a person without warrant if he has reasonable cause to suspect that that person is or has been committing an offence under this section.

(6) For the purpose of arresting a person under the power conferred by subsection (5) above a constable may enter (if need be by force) any place where that person is or where the constable, with reasonable cause, suspects him to be.

(7) Subsection (6) above does not extend to Scotland and nothing in that subsection shall affect any rule of law in Scotland concerning the right of a constable to enter any premises for any purpose.".

(3) For sections 6 to 12 of the 1972 Act there are substituted the sections set out in Schedule 8.

(4) An offence under section 7(4) set out in Schedule 8 shall be included among the offences involving discretionary disqualification (within the meaning of Part III of the 1972 Act).

Increase of
penalty for
failure to stop,
etc.

26.—(1) In Schedule 4 to the 1972 Act, in the entry relating to section 25(4) (failure to stop, etc., after accident), for " £100 " there is substituted " £1,000 ".

(2) Subsection (1) does not apply to offences committed before the commencement of this section.

Compulsory
wearing of
seat belts.
1972 c. 20.

27.—(1) After section 33 of the Road Traffic Act 1972 there shall be inserted the following section : —

"Wearing of
seat belts.
33A.—(1) The Secretary of State may make regulations requiring, subject to such exceptions as may be prescribed, persons who are driving or riding in motor vehicles on a road to wear seat belts of such description as may be prescribed.

(2) Regulations under this section—

(*a*) may make different provision in relation to different classes of vehicles, different descriptions of persons and different circumstances ;

(*b*) shall include exceptions for—

(i) the users of vehicles constructed or adapted for the delivery of goods or mail to consumers or addressees, as the case may be, while engaged in making local rounds of deliveries ;

(ii) the drivers of vehicles while performing a manoeuvre which includes reversing ;

(ii) any person holding a valid certificate signed by a medical practitioner to the effect that it is inadvisable on medical grounds for him to wear a seat belt ;

(*c*) may make any prescribed exceptions subject to such conditions as may be prescribed ; and

(*d*) may prescribe cases in which a fee of a prescribed amount may be charged on an application for any certificate required as a condition of any prescribed exception.

(3) Any person who drives or rides in a motor vehicle in contravention of regulations under this section shall be guilty of an offence ; but notwithstanding any enactment or rule of law no person other than the person actually committing the contravention shall be guilty of an offence by reason of the contravention.

(4) If the holder of any such certificate as is referred to in subsection (2)(*b*) above is informed by a constable that he may be prosecuted for an offence under subsection (3) above, he shall not, in proceedings for that offence, be entitled to rely on the exception afforded to him by the certificate unless—

(*a*) it is produced to the constable at the time he is so informed ; or

(*b*) within five days after the date on which he is so informed, it is produced at such police station as he may have specified to the constable.

(5) Regulations under this section requiring the wearing of seat belts by persons riding in motor vehicles shall not apply to children under the age of fourteen years (to whom the next following section applies).".

(2) In section 169 of the Road Traffic Act 1972 (forgery of documents, etc.) in subsection (2) (documents to which that section applies) after paragraph (*b*) there shall be inserted the following paragraph :— 1972 c. 20.

" (*bb*) any certificate required as a condition of any exception prescribed under section 33A of this Act ; ".

(3) In section 199 of the Road Traffic Act 1972 (exercise of regulation-making powers and Parliamentary control) the following subsection is inserted after subsection (2)—

" (2A) The following provisions apply to regulations made under section 33A above—

(a) when the Secretary of State proposes to make the first regulations under that section he shall lay before each House of Parliament a statement explaining his proposals ; and

(b) no draft of those first regulations shall be laid before Parliament for approval under subsection (4) below until after the expiration of the period of three months beginning with the day on which the statement was laid (or, if the statement was laid on different days, with the later of the two days) ; and

(c) at the end of the period of three years beginning with the day on which the first regulations under that section came into force, all regulations in force under that section shall expire unless their continuation in force has been approved by a resolution of each House of Parliament."

(4) In Part I of Schedule 4 to the Road Traffic Act 1972 (prosecution and punishment of offences) after the entry relating to section 33 there shall be inserted the following entry:—

" 33A. Driving or riding in a   Summarily.   £50   —   —   Sections 181
motor vehicle in con-   and 183
travention of regulations   apply."
requiring wearing of
seat belts.

Restriction on carrying children in the front of motor vehicles.

28.—(1) After section 33 of the 1972 Act there is inserted, after the section inserted by section 27, the following section—

"Restriction on carrying children in the front of motor vehicles.

33B.—(1) Except as provided by regulations a person shall not, without reasonable excuse, drive a motor vehicle on a road when there is in the front of the vehicle a child under the age of fourteen years who is not wearing a seat belt in conformity with regulations.

(2) It is an offence for a person to drive a motor vehicle in contravention of subsection (1) above.

(3) Provision may be made by regulations—

(a) excepting from the prohibition in subsection (1) above children of any prescribed description, vehicles of a prescribed class or the driving of vehicles in such circumstances as may be prescribed ;

(b) defining in relation to any class of vehicle what part of the vehicle is to be regarded as the front of the vehicle for the purposes of that subsection ;

(c) prescribing for the purposes of that subsection the descriptions of seat belt to be worn by children of any prescribed description and the manner in which such a belt is to be fixed and used.

(4) In this section—

" regulations " means regulations made by the Secretary of State under this section ; and

" seat belt " includes any description of restraining device for a child and any reference to wearing a seat belt shall be construed accordingly.".

(2) In Part I of Schedule 4 to the 1972 Act (prosecution and punishment of offences), after the entry relating to section 33A, there is inserted—

| " 33B. | Driving motor vehicle with child in the front not wearing seat belt. | Summarily. | £50 | — | — | Sections 181 and 183 apply." |

29.—(1) After section 84(4) of the 1972 Act (under which a person may drive a vehicle without a licence if he has previously held a licence to drive vehicles of that class and has applied for and is entitled to obtain such a licence) there is inserted—

Persons entitled to drive when licence applied for.

" (4A) The Secretary of State may by regulations provide that subsection (4) above shall also apply (where the requirements of that subsection are otherwise met) in the case of a person who has not previously held a licence to drive vehicles of the relevant class.

Regulations under this subsection shall, if not previously revoked, expire at the end of the period of one year beginning with the day on which they came into operation.".

(2) In the words in parenthesis in section 199(2) of that Act (exceptions from the duty to consult before making regulations) after " section " there is inserted " 84(4A) or ".

30.—(1) In this Part " the 1972 Act " means the Road Traffic Act 1972.

Interpretation of Part IV and consequential and minor amendments.
1972 c. 20.

(2) Sections 19 to 21 shall be construed as if they were contained in Part III of the 1972 Act.

(3) The 1972 Act and section 56 of the Criminal Justice Act 1967 shall have effect subject to the consequential and minor amendments specified in Schedule 9.

1967 c. 80.

PART IV
Commencement of
Part IV.

31.—(1) With the exception of section 29, the provisions of this Part come into force on such day as the Secretary of State may appoint by order made by statutory instrument.

(2) Different days may be appointed under this section for different purposes.

PART V

MISCELLANEOUS AND GENERAL

Miscellaneous

Road humps.

32.—(1) The provisions of Schedule 10 have effect with respect to road humps.

(2) This section and Schedule 10 come into force on such day as the Secretary of State may appoint by order made by statutory instrument, and different days may be so appointed for different purposes.

New basis of
vehicle excise
duty for
goods vehicles.

33.—(1) The duty payable under section 1 of the 1971 Act in respect of goods vehicles on licences taken out on or after such day as Parliament may hereafter determine shall be charged in accordance with the following provisions of this section.

(2) The factors determining the rates of the duty to be charged in respect of goods vehicles of an unladen weight exceeding 30 hundredweight which fall within both—

(*a*) a class to which the Plating and Testing Regulations apply ; and

(*b*) a description in the Tables set out in Part I of Schedule 11 to this Act,

shall be those shown in those Tables and, if or to the extent that Parliament so determines, the additional factors set out in Part II of that Schedule.

(3) The rate of duty to be charged in respect of goods vehicles of an unladen weight exceeding 30 hundredweight which do not fall within a class to which the Plating and Testing Regulations apply shall be the lowest rate which would be chargeable in accordance with Table 1 in Part I of Schedule 11 to this Act if duty were so chargeable.

(4) The rates of duty to be charged in respect of goods vehicles of an unladen weight exceeding 30 hundredweight which do not comply with Construction and Use Regulations but are authorised by an order under section 42 of the 1972 Act to be used on roads shall be—

(*a*) if they fall within a class specified by an order of the Secretary of State made for the purposes of this paragraph, the highest rate that would be chargeable in accordance with Table 2 in Part I of Schedule 11 to this Act if duty were so chargeable ; and

(b) in any other case, the lowest rate which would be chargeable in accordance with Table 1 in that Part of that Schedule if duty were so chargeable.

(5) The rates of duty chargeable in respect of showman's goods vehicles and farmer's goods vehicles (both as defined in Schedule 4 to the 1971 Act) of an unladen weight exceeding 30 hundredweight shall be percentages of a rate or rates chargeable in accordance with the Tables in Part I of Schedule 11 to this Act.

(6) Duty in respect of vehicles of an unladen weight not exceeding 30 hundredweight shall be charged in accordance with Schedule 5 to the 1971 Act.

(7) An order for the purposes of subsection (4)(a) above shall be made by statutory instrument, but no such order shall be made unless a draft of it has been laid before Parliament and approved by resolution of each House of Parliament.

34.—(1) In section 33 and Schedule 11—

" articulated vehicle " means a mechanically propelled vehicle to which a trailer may be attached so that part of the trailer is superimposed upon the vehicle and when the trailer is uniformly loaded not less than twenty per cent of the weight of its load is borne by the vehicle ; Interpretation of s. 33 and Schedule 11.

" goods vehicle " means a mechanically propelled vehicle constructed or adapted for use and used for the conveyance of goods or burden of any description ;

" the Construction and Use Regulations " means regulations under section 40 of the 1972 Act ;

" the Plating and Testing Regulations " means regulations under section 45 of the 1972 Act ;

" rigid goods vehicle " means a goods vehicle which is not an articulated vehicle ;

" the 1971 Act " means the Vehicles (Excise) Act 1971 ; and   1971 c. 10.

" the 1972 Act " means the Road Traffic Act 1972.   1972 c. 20.

(2) For the purposes of this section, section 33 and Schedule 11—

(a) the gross weight of any vehicle is the maximum laden weight for the vehicle as shown on the relevant plate ; and

(b) the train weight of an articulated vehicle is the maximum laden weight for the vehicle together with any trailer which may be drawn by it, as shown on the relevant plate ;

and the relevant plate is the plate with which the vehicle is required to be equipped by the Construction and Use Regulations and, if so required to be equipped with a plate showing particulars determined under the Plating and Testing Regulations, that plate.

(3) The Secretary of State may by regulations—

(a) substitute different definitions for those contained in subsection (2) ; and

(b) require axles of such descriptions as may be specified in the regulations to be disregarded for all or any of the purposes of Schedule 11.

(4) Regulations under subsection (3) shall be made by statutory instrument which shall be subject to annulment in pursuance of a resolution of either House of Parliament.

Charges for licensing of cabs and cab drivers.
1869 c. 115.

35.—(1) In section 6 of the Metropolitan Public Carriage Act 1869 (licensing of cabs) the words " at such price " are omitted and for the words from " such uniform sum " to " prescribe " there are substituted the words " such sum as the person granting the licence may, with the approval of the Secretary of State, determine, and different sums may be so determined with respect to different descriptions of vehicle".

(2) In section 8 of the Metropolitan Public Carriage Act 1869 (licensing of cab drivers) the words " at such price " are omitted and for the words from " such sum " to " prescribe " there are substituted the words " such sum as the person granting the licence may, with the approval of the Secretary of State, determine, and different sums may be so determined with respect to different descriptions of licence ".

1976 c. 57.

1847 c. 89.

(3) Where section 70 of the Local Government (Miscellaneous Provisions) Act 1976 (fees for vehicle and operator's licences) is not in force in the area of a district council, the sums to be paid for a licence granted by the council under section 37 of the Town Police Clauses Act 1847 (licensing of cabs outside London) shall be such as the council may determine, and different sums may be so determined with respect to different descriptions of vehicle ; and the sums so determined shall be such as appear to the council to be sufficient in the aggregate to cover in whole or in part—

(a) the reasonable cost of the carrying out by or on behalf of the district council of inspections of hackney carriages for the purpose of determining whether any such licence should be granted or renewed ;

(b) the reasonable cost of providing hackney carriage stands; and

(c) any reasonable administrative or other costs in connection with the foregoing and with the control and supervision of hackney carriages.

(4) This section does not extend to Scotland.

(5) This section comes into force on such day as the Secretary of State may by order made by statutory instrument, appoint, and different days may be so appointed for different purposes.

36.—(1) Where it appears to the Secretary of State that it Grants to would be in the interests of any locality or of all or some of its assist the inhabitants for facilities to be provided in that locality or else- provision of where for or in connection with the carriage of freight by inland freight haulage waterway or the loading or unloading of freight carried or in- by inland tended to be carried by inland waterway, he may make grants waterway. in accordance with this section towards the provision of such facilities.

(2) Grants under this section shall be made towards capital expenditure which is to be incurred in providing such facilities, and the facilities may, without prejudice to the generality of subsection (1) above, include cargo-carrying craft, inland waterway terminals, depots, access roads and equipment for use in connection with the carriage, loading or unloading of freight.

(3) Grants under this section shall be made in pursuance of an application made to the Secretary of State by the person who intends to provide the facilities and shall be supported by evidence that the navigation authority have given that person their approval for the provision by him of the facilities to which the application relates.

(4) The Secretary of State may, in making a grant under this section, impose such terms and conditions as he thinks fit.

37. In section 67 of the Transport Act 1962 (byelaws for Railway etc. railways and railway shipping services) for subsection (3) there byelaws: is substituted the following subsection— increase in penalties.

" (3) Any byelaws made under this section may 1962 c. 46. provide—

(a) in the case of byelaws made by virtue of subsection (1) above, that any person contravening them shall be liable on summary conviction to a penalty not exceeding £200 for each offence ; and

PART V

(b) in the case of byelaws made by virtue of sub-section (2) above, that any person contravening them shall be liable on summary conviction to a fine not exceeding £50 for each offence and, in the case of such a contravention which continues after conviction, to a fine not exceeding £10 for each day on which the offence so continues.".

Fires caused by railway engines.
1905 c. 11.

38.—(1) In section 1 of the Railway Fires Act 1905 (liability of railway companies to make good damage to crops caused by their engines), in subsection (3) for the words " two hundred pounds " there is substituted " £3,000 or such greater sum as may for the time being be prescribed by order made by the Secretary of State " ; and after that subsection there is inserted the following—

" (3A) An order under subsection (3) above shall be made by statutory instrument which shall be subject to annulment in pursuance of a resolution of either House of Parliament.

(3B) In the application of subsection (3) above to Northern Ireland for the reference to the Secretary of State there shall be substituted a reference to the Department of the Environment for Northern Ireland and any order made by the Department under that subsection—

(a) shall be made by statutory rule for the purposes of the Statutory Rules (Northern Ireland) Order 1979 ; and

(b) shall be subject to negative resolution as defined by section 41(6) of the Interpretation Act (Northern Ireland) 1954 as if it were a statutory instrument within the meaning of that Act."

1923 c. 27.

(2) In section 2 of the Railway Fires Act (1905) Amendment Act 1923 the words " not exceeding the said sum of two hundred pounds " are hereby repealed.

Amendment of Schedules 7 and 8 to the Public Passengers Vehicles Act 1981.
1981 c. 14.
1968 c. 73.
1980 c. 34.

39. In the Public Passenger Vehicles Act 1981—

(a) in Schedule 7 (consequential amendments), paragraph 24 is omitted ;

(b) in Schedule 8 (repeals)—

(i) in the entry relating to the Transport Act 1968 the words " In section 145, subsection (2) " are omitted, and

(ii) in the entry relating to the Transport Act 1980 after the words " In Schedule 5, Part I " there are inserted the words " (except paragraph 13) " and for the words " the Minibus Act 1977 and the Transport Act 1978 " there are substituted the words " and the

Minibus Act 1977 and paragraphs 2 to 4 of the entry   PART V
relating to the Transport Act 1978.".

General

40.—(1) The enactments mentioned in Schedule 12 are Repeals.
repealed to the extent specified in the third column of that
Schedule.

(2) Part I of that Schedule has effect as from the day appointed
by the Secretary of State for the purposes of section 5.

(3) Part II of that Schedule has effect as from the day appointed by the Secretary of State under section 15(1), except for
the repeal of the entry for the National Ports Council in Part II of
Schedule 1 to the House of Commons Disqualification Act 1975 1975 c. 24.
which comes into force on the Council ceasing to exist.

(4) Part III of that Schedule so far as relates to—

    (*a*) the Railway Fires Act (1905) Amendment Act 1923 ; 1923 c. 27.
    and

    (*b*) the Public Passenger Vehicles Act 1981,   1981 c. 14.

comes into force on the passing of this Act and otherwise
comes into force on such day as the Secretary of State may
appoint by order made by statutory instrument and different
days may be so appointed for different purposes.

41.—(1) The following provisions of this Act extend to Northern
Northern Ireland—   Ireland.

    (*a*) Part I ;

    (*b*) Part II, except—

        (i) in Schedule 3, paragraphs 7 and 19 ;

        (ii) in Schedule 4, paragraphs 1, 5 to 9 and 15 ;

    (*c*) Section 38 ;

    (*d*) Part I of Schedule 12, and section 40 so far as relates
    to that Part ;

    (*e*) the repeal by Part II of Schedule 12 of the entry for
    the National Ports Council in Part II of Schedule 1
    to the House of Commons Disqualification Act 1975,
    and section 40 so far as it relates to that repeal ;

    (*f*) Part III of Schedule 12 and section 40 so far as relating
    to the Railway Fires Act (1905) Amendment Act 1923 c. 27.
    1923 ;

    (*g*) this section and sections 42 and 43.

(2) The other provisions of this Act do not extend to
Northern Ireland.

B

PART V
1974 c. 28.

(3) An Order in Council made under paragraph 1(1)(*b*) of Schedule 1 to the Northern Ireland Act 1974 which contains a statement that its purposes correspond to those of sections 27 and 28 of this Act shall be subject to annulment in pursuance of a resolution of either House of Parliament instead of the order or a draft of the order being subject to the procedure set out in paragraph 1(4) or (5) of that Schedule.

Expenses.

42. Expenses incurred by any government department in consequence of the provisions of this Act shall be defrayed out of money provided by Parliament.

Short title.

43. This Act may be cited as the Transport Act 1981.

SCHEDULES

SCHEDULE 1 Section 4.

PROVISIONS SUPPLEMENTING SECTIONS 1 TO 3

Pensions

1.—(1) The Secretary of State may make such orders under section 74 of the Transport Act 1962 (power to make provision about pensions in the nationalised transport industry) in relation to related companies as he could make if those companies were subsidiaries of the Railways Board. 1962 c. 46.

(2) Except on the application of a related company which is not a subsidiary of the Board, no order shall be made by virtue of this paragraph which has the effect of placing the company or any of its subsidiaries in any worse position ; but for this purpose a related company or a subsidiary shall not be regarded as being placed in a worse position because an order provides that any changes in a pension scheme are not to be effected without the consent of the Secretary of State.

(3) An order such as is mentioned in sub-paragraph (2) which is made without the application of the related company shall not be invalid because it does not have the effect of securing that the related company and its subsidiaries are not placed in any worse position, but except in so far as the related company approves the effect of the order the Secretary of State shall as soon as may be make the necessary amending order.

(4) Sub-paragraphs (2) and (3) above have effect only in relation to orders made after such day as may be appointed for the purposes of this paragraph by order made by statutory instrument by the Secretary of State, and different days may be so appointed in relation to different related companies.

(5) Where an order (the " first order ") applying to a company has been made under section 74 and at the time when it was made the company was a subsidiary of the Railways Board, the order shall not apply to that company when it ceases to be such a subsidiary except where an order made (at any time) by virtue of this paragraph provides for the first order to continue to apply to the related company.

(6) An order made by virtue of this paragraph may, in particular, authorise the Railways Board or any subsidiary of the Board—

    (*a*) to transfer liabilities and obligations under a pension scheme in relation to some (but not all) of the participants in that scheme to another pension scheme (the " other scheme ") ; and

    (*b*) to divide or apportion a pension fund held for the purposes of the scheme between that scheme and the other scheme.

(7) In this paragraph " participant ", in relation to a pension scheme, means—

>   (*a*) in relation to a scheme under which benefits are or will be receivable as of right, a person who has pension rights under the scheme (whether he has contributed or not) ; and

>   (*b*) in relation to a scheme under which benefits are not or will not be receivable as of right, a person who (whether he is referred to in the scheme as a member, contributor or otherwise) has contributed under the scheme and has pension rights thereunder.

(8) Section 57 of the Transport Act 1980 (power of Secretary of State to direct that certain payments in respect of transfer values are to be ignored for the purposes of certain provisions of Part III of that Act) shall have effect as if the reference to a subsidiary of the Railways Board included a reference to a related company.

(9) In this paragraph " related company " means a company in which the Railways Board have, or at any time have had, a beneficial interest (either directly or through nominees or subsidiaries) in not less than 20 per cent. of the issued ordinary share capital of the company.

Transport police

2.—(1) The Railways Board may make an agreement with Sealink or the harbours company for making available the services of the British Transport Police Force to Sealink and any of its subsidiaries or to the harbours company and any of its subsidiaries, for such period, to such extent and on such terms as may be specified in the agreement.

(2) Where such an agreement has been made members of the British Transport Police Force shall, notwithstanding the provisions of any other enactment but subject to the terms of the agreement, have the same powers to act as constables in relation to the premises of, and matters connected with or affecting, the company concerned as they would have if those premises belonged to, or those matters were connected with or affected, the Railways Board.

(3) In this section " the British Transport Police Force " means the force established by a scheme made under section 69 of the Transport Act 1962.

Charges

3.—(1) The harbours company shall, in the exercise of statutory powers and duties at a harbour which it is engaged in improving, maintaining or managing, have power to make such reasonable charges for its services and facilities as it thinks fit.

(2) This paragraph does not apply in relation to—

>   (*a*) ship, passenger and goods dues ; or

>   (*b*) charges ascribable to the running of a ferry service in or from a harbour ;

and does not authorise the making of any charge in a case where   SCH. 1
an enactment relating to any of the company's harbours expressly
provides for freedom from charges or otherwise prohibits the making
of any charge.

(3) The provisions of sections 27 to 48 of the Harbours, Docks 1847 c. 27.
and Piers Clauses Act 1847 (which provide for various matters connected with liability for and collection of the rates to be taken by
undertakers) as incorporated with or applied by any enactment relating to any of the company's harbours apply to charges under this
paragraph as if they were rates payable under that enactment.

Stamp duty

4.—(1) Stamp duty shall not be chargeable under section 47 of the
Finance Act 1973 in respect of—   1973 c. 51.

    (*a*) the formation of a subsidiary of the Railways Board ; or

    (*b*) any increase in the capital of such a subsidiary ;

if the transaction concerned is certified by the Treasury as satisfying
the requirements of sub-paragraphs (2) and (3) below.

(2) A transaction satisfies the requirements of this sub-paragraph
if it is effected solely for the purpose—

    (*a*) of facilitating the eventual disposal under section 1 of this
        Act of any part of the Board's undertaking or of any
        property, rights or liabilities ; or

    (*b*) of complying with a direction given by the Secretary of State
        under section 3 of this Act.

(3) A transaction satisfies the requirements of this sub-paragraph
if—

    (*a*) it is entered into solely in connection with a transfer to be
        effected by section 7(6) of the Transport Act 1968, takes 1968 c. 73.
        place on or before the transfer date and does not give rise to
        an excess of capital ; or

    (*b*) it consists of the conversion of loan stock into share capital
        or the issue of shares in satisfaction of a debt owed by the
        subsidiary to the Railways Board or to another of their
        subsidiaries.

(4) In this paragraph " issued capital " means issued share capital
or loan capital ; and for the purposes of this paragraph a transaction
gives rise to an excess of capital if—

    (*a*) in a case falling within sub-paragraph (1)(*a*) above the total
        issued capital of the subsidiary exceeds, on the transfer date,
        the total value of the assets less liabilities transferred ; or

    (*b*) in a case falling within sub-paragraph (1)(*b*) above the aggre-
        gate amount of the increase of issued capital of the sub-
        sidiary exceeds, on that date, that total value.

Provision of services for related companies

5. The Railways Board may provide for any related company
(within the meaning of paragraph 1 above) any of the services
which they have power to provide for any of their subsidiaries.

Leases of vessels

6. Where, immediately before the commencement of this Part of this Act, any vessel is the subject of a lease granted to the Railways Board and of a sub-lease granted by the Board to Sealink, the sub-lease shall be taken to have been validly granted by the Board and the lease and sub-lease shall continue to have effect as if this Part of this Act had not been passed.

This paragraph applies equally where the lease and sub-lease were granted after, but in pursuance of an agreement entered into before, the commencement of this Part.

Repeal of powers to provide shipping services and to provide and manage hotels

7.—(1) If at any time Sealink ceases to be a subsidiary of the Railways Board the Secretary of State shall by order repeal the Railway Shipping Acts.

(2) If at any time the Board cease to provide and manage hotels (either themselves or through a subsidiary) the Secretary of State shall by order repeal subsection (2) (power to provide and manage hotels) of section 50 of the Transport Act 1968 and make such consequential amendments in subsection (4) of that section as he considers appropriate.

1968 c. 73.

(3) In this paragraph " the Railway Shipping Acts " means—

1962 c. 46.
  (a) the enactments so described in section 5 of the Transport Act 1962 ;

1967 c. xxx.
  (b) section 47 of the British Railways Act 1967 ; and

  (c) subsections (1) and (3)(a) of section 5 of the 1962 Act.

(4) An order under this paragraph shall be made by statutory instrument.

(5) Notwithstanding the repeal of the Railway Shipping Acts under this paragraph, the Board shall continue to have power to provide vessels and shipping services for the carriage by sea of rail freight wagons.

(6) The Board shall not exercise their powers under sub-paragraph (5) above to provide shipping services except with the consent of the Secretary of State ; and any consent under this paragraph may be given subject to such conditions as the Secretary of State thinks fit to impose.

Local enactments

8.—(1) Where he considers it necessary or expedient to do so in consequence of, or of anything done under, this Act, the Secretary of State may by order—

  (a) repeal any local enactment which in his opinion has ceased to have effect ; or

  (b) make such amendments in any local enactment as he thinks appropriate.

(2) An order under this paragraph shall be made by statutory instrument which shall be subject to annulment in pursuance of a resolution of either House of Parliament.

SCHEDULE 2

FURTHER PROVISIONS WITH RESPECT TO THE CONSTITUTION AND PROCEEDINGS OF ASSOCIATED BRITISH PORTS AND RELATED MATTERS

Preliminary

1. In this Schedule " director " means a director of Associated British Ports.

Remuneration and other payments

2.—(1) The remuneration and allowances payable to directors by Associated British Ports shall be determined by the Holding Company.

(2) The payment by Associated British Ports to or in respect of a former director of any pension or compensation for loss of office shall be subject to the approval of the Holding Company.

Resignation and vacation of office

3.—(1) A director may resign his office by notice in writing to Associated British Ports.

(2) The office of director is vacated if the director—

  (*a*) becomes bankrupt or makes an arrangement with his creditors, or in Scotland has his estate sequestrated or makes a trust deed for behoof of his creditors or a composition contract ; or

  (*b*) becomes of unsound mind ; or

  (*c*) is absent from meetings of the directors for a period of more than six months without the permission of the directors.

Proceedings of the directors

4.—(1) Subject to any rules which may be prescribed by the Holding Company, the directors may regulate their own procedure.

(2) Unless the directors determine otherwise, the quorum necessary for the transaction of business by them is three.

Chairman and deputy chairman

5.—(1) The directors may elect a chairman of their meetings and determine the period for which he is to hold office.

(2) If the directors elect a chairman they may also elect a deputy chairman and determine the period for which he is to hold office.

Committees of directors

6.—(1) The directors may delegate any of their powers to a committee consisting of one or more directors.

(2) Subject to any rules which may be prescribed by the directors, such a committee may regulate its own procedure and may elect a chairman of its meetings.

Executive directors

7.—(1) The directors may appoint one or more of their number as executive directors.

(2) Such an appointment shall be for such period and on such terms as the directors think fit, but shall determine automatically if the person appointed ceases to be a director.

(3) The directors may delegate any of their powers to an executive director on such terms and subject to such restrictions as they think fit.

(4) An appointment as executive director may be revoked at any time by the directors, but without prejudice to any claim for damages for breach of contract.

Secretary

8.—(1) The directors shall appoint a secretary of Associated British Ports on such terms as to remuneration and otherwise as the directors think fit.

(2) A secretary so appointed may be removed by the directors at any time, but without prejudice to any claim for damages for breach of contract.

9. The fixing of the common seal of Associated British Ports shall be authenticated by the signature of the secretary or some other person authorised by the directors to act for that purpose.

Auditors

10.—(1) The auditors of Associated British Ports shall be appointd by the Holding Company for such period as the Holding Company may determine but, without prejudice to any claim for damages for breach of contract, may be removed by the Holding Company at any time.

(2) The amounts payable by Associated British Ports to its auditors in respect of remuneration and expenses shall be determined by the Holding Company.

Validity of proceedings notwithstanding formal defects

11.—(1) The validity of proceedings of the directors is not affected by any vacancy among the directors.

(2) Acts done by the directors, by a committee of directors or by any person acting as director are valid notwithstanding that it is afterwards discovered—

    (a) that there was some defect in the appointment of any such director or person acting as director ; or

    (b) that any such director or person acting as director was disqualified from acting on grounds of interest or had ceased to hold office as director by virtue of paragraph 3(2).

SCHEDULE 3

Powers of Associated British Ports

Preliminary

1. Each of the powers conferred on Associated British Ports by this Schedule is in addition to, and not in derogation of, any other power conferred on Associated British Ports by this Schedule or by any other enactment.

Operation of harbours and provision of port facilities

2. Associated British Ports has power to operate its harbours and to provide port facilities at them.

Consignment and carriage of goods

3.—(1) Associated British Ports may consign goods on behalf of other persons to or from or on routes through its harbours.

(2) Associated British Ports may carry goods by road on behalf of other persons to or from its harbours.

Activities as ship's agent

4. Associated British Ports may carry on at its harbours the activities of a ship's agent.

Storage of goods

5. Associated British Ports may provide facilities for the storage of goods.

Development of land

6.—(1) Associated British Ports may develop in such manner as it thinks fit land belonging to it or to any of its subsidiaries.

(2) Associated British Ports may in particular—

(a) develop for use by other persons land belonging to it or to any of its subsidiaries which is not otherwise required for the purposes of its business ; or

(b) where the use of such land for the purposes of its business can be combined with its use by other persons, develop the land by constructing or adapting buildings on it for use wholly or partly by other persons,

with a view to the disposal of any right or interest in the land or, as the case may be, the buildings or any part of the buildings, after the development is carried out.

(3) Where Associated British Ports proposes under this paragraph to develop any land as mentioned in sub-paragraph (2), it may acquire by agreement adjoining land for the purpose of developing it together with the other land.

(4) Except as provided by sub-paragraph (3), Associated British Ports does not have power to acquire land solely for the purpose of developing it as mentioned in sub-paragraph (2).

Pipelines

7.—(1) Associated British Ports may construct and operate pipelines in Great Britain.

(2) The power conferred by sub-paragraph (1) includes power to construct and operate any works provided in connection with the operation of a pipeline.

(3) Associated British Ports does not have power to acquire land for the purpose of constructing pipelines except—

    (*a*) where the pipeline is, or is to be, mainly on land acquired for other purposes ; or

    (*b*) where the pipeline is required for the purposes of the business of Associated British Ports other than the operation of pipelines.

Incidental amenities and facilities

8.—(1) In places where those using the services and facilities provided by Associated British Ports or any of its subsidiaries may require them, Associated British Ports may provide both for them and for other persons facilities for the purchase and consumption of food and drink and such other amenities and facilities as appear to Associated British Ports appropriate.

(2) Associated British Ports may, at any place where, in the exercise of the power conferred by sub-paragraph (1), it or any of its subsidiaries provides a car park, repair motor vehicles, both for persons using the car park and others, and sell to any such persons petrol, oil, spare parts and accessories for motor vehicles.

Other activities

9. Associated British Ports may carry on any business which in its opinion can advantageously be carried on by reason of the fact that the business—

    (*a*) involves the use of machinery, plant or equipment of a kind used by Associated British Ports or any of its subsidiaries in connection with the operation of its harbours ; or

    (*b*) requires skills which employees of Associated British Ports or any of its subsidiaries have in connection with the operation of its harbours.

10.—(1) Associated British Ports may manufacture for sale to any person and repair for any person anything which it considers can advantageously be so manufactured or repaired by reason of the fact that Associated British Ports or any of its subsidiaries has materials or facilities for, or skill in, the manufacture or repair of that thing in connection with its existing activities.

(2) Associated British Ports may sell to any person, and for that purpose purchase, anything which is of a kind which Associated British Ports or any of its subsidiaries purchases in the course of its existing activities.

(3) In this paragraph " existing actvities " includes existing activities carried on by virtue of this paragraph.

11. Associated British Ports may provide for any person technical advice or assistance including research services as respects any matter in which it or any of its subsidiaries has skill or experience.

Acquisition of further harbour undertakings

12.—(1) Associated British Ports may, either alone or together with any other person, provide, maintain or operate harbours additional to those which it or any of its subsidiaries owns or manages by virtue of Part II of the Transport Act 1962 (which 1962 c. 46. provided for the division of the undertaking of the British Transport Commission) or by virtue of a harbour reorganisation scheme under the Harbours Act 1964.   1964 c. 40.

(2) For the purposes of sub-paragraph (1) Associated British Ports may acquire by agreement any harbour undertaking, or any part of such an undertaking.

(3) Associated British Ports may subscribe for or acquire shares or securities of a body corporate which is wholly or mainly engaged, or which it is proposed should become wholly or mainly engaged, in the provision, maintenance or operation of a harbour.

Disposal and discontinuance of parts of Associated British Ports' undertaking, etc.

13.—(1) Associated British Ports may dispose of any part of its undertaking, or any property, which in its opinion is not required by it for the purposes of its business.

(2) Associated British Ports may dispose of or discontinue any part of its undertaking carried on by virtue of paragraph 9 or 10.

(3) Associated British Ports may dispose of or discontinue any part of its undertaking acquired under paragraph 12, and may dispose of any shares or securities subscribed for or acquired under that paragraph.

(4) The powers of disposal conferred by this paragraph include power—

(*a*) to dispose of property absolutely or for a term of years ;

(*b*) to dispose of a right in, or interest over, property.

Power to promote and oppose Bills

14.—(1) Associated British Ports may promote Bills in Parliament and may oppose any Bill in Parliament.

(2) The power conferred by sub-paragraph (1) is in lieu of any power to promote or oppose Bills which Associated British Ports might otherwise possess as successor to the persons carrying on any undertaking, and, in particular, the persons carrying on any under-taking transferred to the British Transport Commission by the Transport Act 1947, but nothing in this sub-paragraph affects any 1947 c. 49. power exercisable by Associated British Ports as successor to apply for orders and schemes, and oppose applications for orders and schemes, including orders and schemes subject to special parliamentary procedure.

(3) In the application of this paragraph to Scotland, " Bill in Parliament " includes an order under the Private Legislation Procedure (Scotland) Act 1936.

Training, education and research

15.—(1) Associated British Ports may do anything it thinks fit for the purpose of advancing—

(a) the skill of its employees and those of its subsidiaries ; or

(b) the efficiency and manner in which the equipment of Associated British Ports and its subsidiaries is operated,

including making, or assisting the making, of provision for training and education.

(2) Associated British Ports may do anything which appears to it practicable or desirable for the purpose of—

(a) promoting research into matters affecting, or arising out of, the activities of Associated British Ports and its subsidiaries ; or

(b) turning to account the results of any such research.

Provision of accommodation, etc.

16.—(1) Associated British Ports may provide houses, hostels and other like accommodation for its employees and those of its subsidiaries.

(2) Associated British Ports may make housing loans to such employees to assist them to acquire housing accommodation and may guarantee loans made for housing purposes to such employees by building societies and other bodies.

Pensions

17.—(1) Associated British Ports may pay pensions and enter into obligations under pension schemes.

(2) Associated British Ports may lend money to be applied for the purposes of a pension scheme under which it, or any of its subsidiaries, pays employer's contributions or is subject to any other obligations.

Acquisition of land

18.—(1) Associated British Ports has power to acquire land for the purposes of its business.

(2) Sub-paragraph (1) is subject to paragraphs 6(4) and 7(3).

(3) Where it is proposed to dispose of any land belonging to Associated British Ports or any of its subsidiaries, Associated British Ports may acquire by agreement adjoining land for the purpose of disposing of it together with that land.

Compulsory purchase of land

19.—(1) Subject to sub-paragraph (2), the Secretary of State may authorise Associated British Ports to purchase compulsorily any land in Great Britain which it requires for the purposes of its business ; and the Acquisition of Land (Authorisation Procedure) Act 1946 shall apply as if Associated British Ports were a local authority within the meaning of that Act and as if this Act had been in force immediately before the commencement of that Act.

(2) This paragraph does not authorise Associated British Ports to purchase compulsorily—

> (a) land required for the purposes of a business carried on by a subsidiary of Associated British Ports other than a wholly-owned subsidiary ;
>
> (b) land required for the purposes of a business or activity carried on by virtue of paragraph 3(2), 4, 9 or 10 ;
>
> (c) land required for the purpose of providing facilities for the storage of goods other than goods which have been or are to be loaded or unloaded in or carried through one of Associated British Ports' harbours ; or
>
> (d) land which Associated British Ports has power to acquire by agreement under paragraph 6(3) or 18(3).

(3) Subject to sub-paragraph (4), the power of purchasing land compulsorily in this paragraph includes power to acquire an easement or other right over land by the creation of a new right.

(4) Sub-paragraph (3) does not apply to an easement or other right over any land which forms part of a common, open space or fuel or field garden allotment within the meaning of the Acquisition of Land (Authorisation Procedure) Act 1946. 1946 c. 49.

(5) In the application of this paragraph to Scotland—

> (a) for any reference to the Acquisition of Land (Authorisation Procedure) Act 1946 there is substituted a reference to the Acquisition of Land (Authorisation Procedure) (Scot- 1947 c. 42. land) Act 1947 ;
>
> (b) for any reference to an easement there is substituted a reference to a servitude ; and
>
> (c) the reference in sub-paragraph (4) to a fuel or field garden allotment is omitted.

Charges

20.—(1) Subject to sub-paragraph (2), Associated British Ports may make such reasonable charges as it thinks fit for services and facilities provided by it or by its subsidiaries.

(2) This paragraph does not authorise—

> (a) the levying of ship, passenger and goods dues within the meaning of the Harbours Act 1964 ; or 1964 c. 40.
>
> (b) the making of a charge in any case where an enactment relating to any of Associated British Ports' harbours expressly provides for freedom from charges or otherwise prohibits the making of any charge.

(3) The provisions of sections 27 to 48 of the Harbours, Docks 1847 c. 27. and Piers Clauses Act 1847 (which provide for various matters connected with liability for and collection of the rates to be taken by the undertakers) as incorporated with or applied by any enactment relating to any of Associated British Ports' harbours apply to charges under this paragraph as if they were rates payable under that enactment.

                                        Borrowing and guarantees

21.—(1) Subject to sub-paragraph (5), Associated British Ports may borrow money for any of the purposes of its business, whether of a capital or revenue nature and including any proposed exercise of the powers conferred by paragraph 12, and may do so in such a manner and on such terms as it considers expedient.

(2) Without prejudice to the generality of sub-paragraph (1), the power conferred by that sub-paragraph may be exercised—

   (a) by the issue of debentures on such terms as Associated British Ports thinks fit ;

   (b) by borrowing from a bank on overdraft ;

   (c) by opening an acceptance credit with a bank or accepting house ;

   (d) by accepting money on deposit.

(3) Subject to sub-paragraph (5), Associated British Ports may, for the purposes of its business, give a guarantee for the benefit of any person for the purposes of an undertaking carried on by him or, where that person is a body corporate, any undertaking carried on by a subsidiary of that body corporate.

(4) Associated British Ports may, by way of security for any of its borrowing or any guarantee given by it, mortgage or charge all or any part of its undertaking, revenues, property or assets (present or future).

(5) The aggregate amount outstanding at any time of—

   (a) the principal of money borrowed by Associated British Ports and its subsidiaries ; and

   (b) guarantees given by Associated British Ports and its subsidiaries,

shall not exceed the limit for the time being set by the Holding Company.

                Restrictions on certain descriptions of financial arrangement

22.—(1) The Holding Company may from time to time impose restrictions on the descriptions of financial arrangement which may be entered into by Associated British Ports and its subsidiaries.

(2) The Holding Company may, in particular, prohibit Associated British Ports and its subsidiaries from entering into specified descriptions of financial arrangement—

   (a) absolutely, or

   (b) without the consent of the Holding Company,

and may set a limit on the aggregate amount of the liabilities which Associated British Ports and its subsidiaries may incur in respect of arrangements of any specified description.

(3) Restrictions imposed under this paragraph may be varied or revoked by the Holding Company from time to time.

General supplementary powers

23. Associated British Ports may purchase, manufacture or repair anything required for the purposes of its business.

24. Associated British Ports may acquire any undertaking or part of an undertaking if the assets of the undertaking or part are wholly or mainly assets which it requires for the purposes of its business.

25. Associated British Ports may, for the purposes of its business, subscribe for or acquire shares or securities of any body corporate.

26. Associated British Ports may, for the purpose of its business, lend money to any person for the purposes of an undertaking carried on by him or, where that person is a body corporate, any undertaking carried on by a subsidiary of that body corporate.

27. Associated British Ports may—

    (a) invest any sums not immediately required for the purposes of its business; and

    (b) turn its resources to account so far as not required for those purposes.

28. Associated British Ports may do all other things which in its opinion are necessary or expedient to facilitate the proper carrying on of its business.

Subsidiaries

29.—(1) Associated British Ports may form and promote, or join with any other person in forming and promoting, a company for carrying on any activities which Associated British Ports has power to carry on.

(2) Associated British Ports may enter into arrangements with a company formed in exercise of the powers conferred by sub-paragraph (1) for the transfer to that company from Associated British Ports or any of its subsidiaries, in such manner and on such terms (including payments by any of the parties to the arrangements to any other of them) as may be provided for by the arrangements, of any property, rights, liabilities or obligations of Associated British Ports or any of its subsidiaries relevant to the carrying on of the activities to be carried on by the company.

Working agreements, etc.

30.—(1) Associated British Ports may enter into an agreement with any person for the carrying on by that person, whether as agent of Associated British Ports or otherwise, of any of the activities which Associated British Ports may itself carry on.

(2) Associated British Ports may enter into arrangements with a person with whom an agreement is made under sub-paragraph (1) for the transfer to that person from Associated British Ports or any of its subsidiaries, in such manner and on such terms (including payments by any of the parties to the arrangements to any other of them) as may be provided for by the arrangements, of any property, rights, liabilities or obligations of Associated British Ports or any of its subsidiaries relevant to the carrying on of the activities to be carried on by that person.

Powers in relation to public transport authorities

31.—(1) Associated British Ports may purchase, manufacture or repair anything required for the purposes of the business of any public transport authority or any subsidiary of such an authority.

(2) Without prejudice to paragraph 30(1), Associated British Ports may enter into an agreement with a public transport authority or with a subsidiary of such an authority for the management, working and use by one party to the agreement of works, land or other property belonging to the other party, and with respect to the rendering of services and pooling of receipts or expenses.

(3) An agreement under sub-paragraph (2) may be entered into notwithstanding that it involves a delegation of functions under any enactment relating to any part of the undertaking of a party to the agreement.

(4) In this paragraph " public transport authority " means the British Railways Board, the British Waterways Board, the London Transport Executive, the Scottish Transport Group and the National Bus Company.

Interpretation

32. In this Schedule—

(a) references to selling and purchasing include references to supplying or obtaining by exchange, hire or hire-purchase ;

(b) references to manufacture include references to construction and production ;

(c) references to repair include references to maintenance ; and

(d) references to goods include references to fish, livestock and animals of all descriptions.

Section 14.

SCHEDULE 4

PROVISIONS SUPPLEMENTING SECTIONS 5 TO 13

PART I

SUPPLEMENTARY AND CONSEQUENTIAL PROVISIONS

Provisions of Harbours Act 1964 and Docks and Harbours Act 1966 applying to Associated British Ports

1964 c. 40.

1.—(1) In the definition of " the Boards " in section 57(1) of the Harbours Act 1964 the words " the British Transport Docks Board " are repealed.

(2) In consequence of sub-paragraph (1) the following provisions apply to Associated British Ports as they apply to harbour authorities generally—

(a) sections 26, 27, 30, 31 and 40 of the Harbours Act 1964 (power to make charges, certain charges to be reasonable, revision of charges and power to impose conditions as to use of harbour services and facilities) ;

(*b*) section 42 of that Act (accounts and reports);   SCH. 4

(*c*) sections 37 and 39 of the Docks and Harbours Act 1966   1966 c. 28.
(acquisition of harbour businesses or securities of bodies
carrying on such businesses).

(3) In section 47 of the Docks and Harbours Act 1966 (policing
of harbour premises by British Transport Police), in subsection (3)
after "section 69 of the Transport Act 1962" there is inserted
"and 'the Boards' has the same meaning as in that section"

Provisions of Transport Act 1962 and Transport Act 1968 continuing to apply to Associated British Ports

2.—(1) Except as provided by the following provisions of this
paragraph, the provisions of the Transport Act 1962 and the Trans-   1962 c. 46.
port Act 1968 relating to the Boards established by the said Act of   1968 c. 73.
1962 no longer apply to Associated British Ports.

(2) The following provisions of the Transport Act 1962 continue
to apply to Associated British Ports—

(*a*) section 1(1) (establishment of the Boards);

(*b*) section 13(1) (powers of manufacture and production) and
section 14(1)(*b*) (power to enter into working agreements),
so far as those provisions confer power on authorities
other than Associated British Ports;

(*c*) section 24(4) (exclusion of certain enactments relating to
accounts, statistics and returns);

(*d*) Part II, sections 67(15) and 81 and paragraph 24 of Schedule
7 (provisions relating to the division of the functions of the
British Transport Commission and consequential matters);

(*e*) section 43(4) and (5) (exclusion of certain enactments relating to railway undertakers);

(*f*) sections 52(4) and 83(7) (which exclude the Boards from the
definition of independent railway undertakings);

(*g*) section 67(16) (power to make bylaws in relation to railways
within a harbour);

(*h*) sections 69 to 71 (transport police);

(*i*) sections 74 and 75 and Part IV of Schedule 7 (pensions).

(3) The following provisions of the Transport Act 1968 continue
to apply to Associated British Ports—

(*a*) section 51(5) and (6) (joint subsidiaries), so far as those
provisions relate to companies which are not subsidiaries of
Associated British Ports, except that the Secretary of State's
power to give directions under subsection (6) is not exercisable with respect to Associated British Ports;

(*b*) section 125 (powers of inspectors of railways);

(*c*) section 141(2) (application of Town and Country Planning
Acts), so far as that provision relates to companies which
are not wholly-owned subsidiaries of Associated British
Ports;

(*d*) section 144 (transfer and disposal of historical records and
relics);

SCH. 4

(e) paragraph 7(1) of Schedule 16 (references to the Boards in certain enactments to include wholly-owned subsidiaries of the Boards).

Restriction on cross-eligibility under existing pensions orders

1962 c. 46.

3.—(1) In this paragraph " pensions order " means an order made under section 74 of the Transport Act 1962 (which confers on the Secretary of State power to make orders about pensions in the nationalised transport industry).

(2) A person who on or after the appointed day leaves or enters the employment of the group consisting of Associated British Ports and its subsidiaries (in this paragraph referred to as " the Ports group ") is not eligible by virtue of any provision of a pensions order made before that day—

(a) to participate in a Ports pension scheme by reason of any employment outside the Ports group ; or

(b) to participate in a pension scheme other than a Ports pension scheme by reason of his employment within the Ports group.

(3) For the purposes of this paragraph the following are Ports pension schemes—

(a) any pension scheme established by the British Transport Docks Board ;

(b) any pension scheme in relation to which the rights, liabilities and functions of the British Transport Commission were transferred to that Board in pursuance of paragraph 14 of Schedule 7 to the Transport Act 1962 ;

(c) any pension scheme in relation to which the responsibility for making payments was transferred to that Board by virtue of paragraph 15 of that Schedule.

Pensions orders made on or after the appointed day

4.—(1) In this paragraph " pensions order " has the same meaning as in paragraph 3.

(2) Subject to the following provisions of this paragraph, the power to make pensions orders is exercisable on and after the appointed day as if the Holding Company were a Board within the meaning of the Transport Act 1962.

(3) Except on the application of the Holding Company, no pensions order shall be made on or after the appointed day which has the effect of placing in any worse position the Holding Company or any subsidiary of that company.

(4) or the purposes of sub-paragraph (3, the Holding Company or a subsidiary shall not be regarded as being placed in a worse position because a pensions order provides that any changes in a pension scheme are not to be effected without the consent of the Secretary of State.

(5) A pensions order such as is mentioned in sub-paragraph (3) SCH. 4 which is made without the application of the Holding Company is not invalid because in fact it does not have the effect of securing that the Holding Company and its subsidiaries are not placed in any worse position, but except in so far as the Holding Company approves the effect of the order the Secretary of State shall as soon as may be make the necessary amending order.

Appointment of members of Local Boards

5.—(1) As from the appointed day the members of the Humber Local Board and the Southampton Local Board shall be appointed by Associated British Ports ; and the Humber and Southampton Orders are accordingly amended as follows.

(2) In Article 11 of each Order (appointment of members)—

(*a*) for the references to the Secretary of State there are substituted references to Associated British Ports ; and

(*b*) references to consultation with the chairman for the time being of the British Transport Docks Board are omitted.

(3) In Article 16(1) of the Humber Order and Article 16(2) of the Southampton Order (notice of resignation) for the reference to the Secretary of State there is substituted a reference to Associated British Ports.

(4) In this paragraph " the Humber Order " means the Humber S.I. 1968/237. Harbour Reorganisation Scheme 1966 Confirmation Order 1967 and " the Southampton Order " means the Southampton Harbour Reorganisation Scheme 1967 Confirmation Order 1968. S.I. 1968/941.

(5) Sub-paragraph (3) applies to any notice of resignation given on or after the appointed day, but subject to that this paragraph does not affect appointments made before the appointed day.

Payments for making up of private streets

6. In section 219 of the Highways Act 1980 (payments to be 1980 c. 66. made by owners of new buildings in respect of street works), in subsection (4)(*i*) (exemption for certain public authorities), the words " the British Transport Docks Board " are repealed.

Taxation

7.—(1) Stamp duty is not chargeable under section 47 of the Fin- 1973 c. 51. ance Act 1973 in respect of an increase in the capital of the Holding Company which is certified by the Treasury as having been effected—

(*a*) for the purpose of complying with the requirements of section 6 ; or

(*b*) in consequence of the exercise of conversion rights attached to convertible shares or securities issued in pursuance of that section.

(2) Section 92(9)(*b*) of the Finance Act 1972 (restriction on 1972 c. 41. surrender of surplus advance corporation tax) and section 28(2) of the Finance Act 1973 (restriction of group relief) shall not apply to the Holding Company as the parent company of Associated British Ports.

Sch. 4

(3) Payments by Associated British Ports under section 11(1) of this Act shall be treated as dividends for the purposes of the enactments relating to corporation tax.

(4) The vesting on the appointed day in the Holding Company of powers in relation to Associated British Ports shall not be regarded as constituting a change in the ownership of Associated British Ports for the purposes of section 483 of the Income and Corporation Taxes Act 1970 (restriction on carry forward of loss relief) or section 101 of the Finance Act 1972 (restriction on carry forward of relief for advance corporation tax).

1970 c. 10.

1972 c. 41.

Application of Trustee Investments Act 1961 to securities of the Holding Company

1961 c. 62.

8. For the purposes of paragraph 3(*b*) of Part IV of Schedule 1 to the Trustee Investments Act 1961 (which excludes securities of a company from trustee status unless the company has paid a dividend in each of the preceding five calendar years) the Holding Company shall be deemed to have paid such a dividend as is mentioned in that provision in the calendar year in which the appointed day falls and in each of the preceding four calendar years.

Wholly-owned subsidiaries of Associated British Ports to be treated as statutory undertakers

1971 c. 78.

1972 c. 52.

9. So far as the activities of any wholly-owned subsidiary of Associated British Ports consist of the carrying on of any such undertaking as is mentioned in the definition of " statutory undertakers " in section 290(1) of the Town and Country Planning Act 1971 or section 275(1) of the Town and Country Planning (Scotland) Act 1972, that subsidiary shall be deemed for the purposes of any enactment relating to statutory undertakers or statutory undertakings to be such an undertaker carrying on such an undertaking.

Part II

Transitional Provisions and Savings

Directors of Associated British Ports

10.—(1) The persons who immediately before the appointed day were members of the British Transport Docks Board shall continue to hold office on and after that day as directors of Associated British Ports as if appointed by the Holding Company on that day for a period corresponding to the unexpired period of their existing appointments and on the same terms, as to remuneration and otherwise, as applied to those appointments, but subject to paragraph 3 of Schedule 2 and to the Holding Company's power of removal.

1975 c. 24.

1975 c. 25.

(2) The repeal by this Act of the entries for the British Transport Docks Board in Part II of Schedule 1 to the House of Commons Disqualification Act 1975 and Part II of Schedule 1 to the Northern Ireland Assembly Disqualification Act 1975 does not affect the operation of those provisions in relation to directors of Associated British Ports holding office by virtue of appointments made before the appointed day.

Chairman and deputy chairman

11. The persons who immediately before the appointed day were chairman and vice-chairman of the British Transport Docks Board hold office on and after that day, so long as they remain directors, as chairman and deputy chairman, respectively, of the directors of Associated British Ports as if elected by the directors under paragraph 5 of Schedule 2 for a period corresponding to the unexpired period of their appointments.

Accounts and annual report

12.—(1) For the purposes of sections 24 and 27(8) of the Transport 1962 c. 46. Act 1962 (accounts and annual report) the accounting year of the British Transport Docks Board then current shall be taken to end with the day before the appointed day.

(2) No amendment or repeal made by this Act affects the operation of those sections in relation to periods before the appointed day.

Profits attributable to periods before the appointed day

13.—(1) The profits of Associated British Ports out of which payments may be made under section 11(1) include accumulated profits attributable to periods before the appointed day.

(2) Dividends paid by subsidiaries of Associated British Ports on or after the appointed day shall be taken into account in ascertaining the profits of Associated British Ports out of which payments may be made under section 11(1), notwithstanding that they are paid wholly or partly out of profits of the subsidiary attributable to periods before the appointed day.

(3) For the purposes of section 39 of the Companies Act 1980 1980 c. 22. (profits available for distribution) sums received by the Holding Company under section 11(1) shall be regarded as profits of the period in which they are received notwithstanding that they are paid by Associated British Ports out of accumulated profits attributable to periods before the appointed day.

Charges

14. Any charges in force immediately before the appointed day in respect of services or facilities provided by the British Transport Docks Board shall as from that day be deemed—

    (a) in the case of ship, passenger and goods dues within the meaning of the Harbours Act 1964, to have been imposed 1964 c. 40. under section 26 of that Act ;

    (b) in the case of other charges, to have been imposed under paragraph 20 of Schedule 3.

Debts owed by harbour authorities to Secretary of State

15. This Act does not affect any liability of a harbour authority in respect of a debt owed by them to the Secretary of State by virtue of section 41 of the Docks and Harbours Act 1966 (power to trans- 1966 c. 28. fer part of commencing capital debt and other debts by harbour revision order or harbour reorganisation scheme) or by virtue of any local Act.

SCH. 4

*Instruments issued by the British
Transport Docks Board*

1962 c. 46.

16. Nothing in this Act affects the operation of paragraph 5 of Schedule 1 to the Transport Act 1962 as respects any document issued before the appointed day and purporting to be an instrument issued by the British Transport Docks Board.

Local and private enactments

17. This Act does not affect the operation of local or private enactments relating to Associated British Ports or any of its harbours, except where—

    (*a*) express provision is made to that effect ; or

    (*b*) an amendment or repeal is made of a provision of a public general Act which is incorporated with or applied by such an enactment.

Sections 15 to 17.

SCHEDULE 5

PROVISIONS SUPPLEMENTING SECTIONS 15 TO 17

PART I

FURTHER PROVISIONS RELATING TO THE DISSOLUTION OF THE NATIONAL PORTS COUNCIL

Duty of Council to facilitate the carrying into effect of section 15 and this Schedule

1. It is the duty of the Council to give to the Secretary of State all such information, to prepare all such documents and to do all such other things as appear to him to be necessary or expedient for facilitating the carrying into effect of section 15 and this Schedule and for enabling him to exercise any functions conferred or imposed on him by or by virtue of that section or this Schedule.

Final accounts of the Council

1964 c. 40.

2.—(1) The Council shall (if they have not done so before the appointed day) comply after that day with subsections (1) to (4) and subsection (7) of section 8 of the Harbours Act 1964 (which relate to the making and publication of periodical reports by the Council and the preparation, audit and publication of their accounts) in relation to their last normal accounting period before the appointed day ; and they shall also comply with those subsections in respect of the interval (if any) between the end of that accounting period and the appointed day, and that interval shall by virtue of this paragraph be an accounting period for the purposes of those sub-sections.

(2) In sub-paragraph (1) " normal accounting period " means an accounting period, within the meaning of the Harbours Act 1964, of not less than twelve months.

(3) The Secretary of State shall lay before each House of Parliament a copy of each report made to him by virtue of sub-paragraph (1), of the statement of accounts attached thereto and of any report on that statement by the auditors.

Disposal of confidential documents belonging to the Council

3.—(1) It is the duty of the Council to set aside any documents belonging to them the disclosure of the contents of which to the Secretary of State would be a breach of confidence and, notwithstanding section 15(1)(*b*), such documents do not vest in the Secretary of State on the appointed day.

(2) References in this paragraph to breach of confidence are to—

   (*a*) the disclosure otherwise than as permitted by section 46 of the Harbours Act 1964 of information furnished to the Council in pursuance of requirements imposed under section 4 or 41 of that Act ; or

   (*b*) the disclosure of information furnished to the Council otherwise than in pursuance of requirements so imposed, being information which in the opinion of the Council ought to be treated as confidential,

not being, in either case, information which the Secretary of State would be entitled to require from any person in exercise of any power conferred on him by this Act or the Harbours Act 1964.

(3) Where a document which is set aside in pursuance of sub-paragraph (1) also contains information which could be disclosed to the Secretary of State without a breach of confidence, the Council shall, if he so directs, extract that information and furnish it to him.

(4) Subject to sub-paragraph (3), documents which are set aside in pursuance of sub-paragraph (1) shall be destroyed or otherwise disposed of by the Council in such manner as the Secretary of State may direct so as to prevent any breach of confidence.

(5) The preceding provisions of this paragraph—

   (*a*) do not apply to documents relating to legal or other proceedings to which the Secretary of State becomes a party on the appointed day in place of the Council ; and

   (*b*) do not affect the Council's duty under paragraph 1.

(6) In this paragraph—

   " document " includes any device in which information is recorded or stored ;

   " information " includes forecasts.

Continuance of Council until residual functions completed to Secretary of State's satisfaction

4.—(1) No amendment or repeal made by this Act affects—

   (*a*) the continuance of the Council for the purposes of paragraphs 1 to 3 or their powers and duties under those paragraphs ; or

(b) the continued operation for those purposes of the provisions of the Harbours Act 1964 relating to the constitution and proceedings of the Council ;

and the Council shall cease to exist when the Secretary of State, being satisfied that their duties under those paragraphs have been completed, so directs by order made by statutory instrument.

(2) Section 15(1)(b) does not affect the continuance of employment with the Council, but on the Council ceasing to exist—

   (a) any contract of employment with the Council then in force shall cease to have effect, except as regards rights previously accrued and liabilities previously incurred ; and

   (b) any rights and liabilities of the Council then existing shall by virtue of this paragraph become rights and liabilities of the Secretary of State.

(3) The Secretary of State shall pay to members of the Council, in respect of the period beginning with the appointed day and ending with the Council ceasing to exist, such remuneration (whether by way of salary or fees) and such allowances as, with the approval of the Minister for the Civil Service, he may determine.

(4) The Secretary of State shall, as soon as possible after determining the amount of any remuneration or allowances payable under sub-paragraph (3), lay a statement of his determination before each House of Parliament.

(5) As from the appointed day, the Secretary of State shall make available to the Council such facilities as the Council or their auditors may reasonably require for performing the duties imposed on them by or by virtue of paragraphs 1 to 3 ; and the remuneration of the auditors and any other expenses incurred by the Council in connection with the performance of those duties on and after the appointed day shall be defrayed by the Secretary of State.

Modification of agreements and documents

5.—(1) Every agreement, other than a contract of employment, to which the Council are a party immediately before the appointed day, whether in writing or not and whether or not of such a nature that rights and liabilities thereunder could be assigned by the Council, has effect as from that date as if—

   (a) the Secretary of State had been a party to the agreement ; and

   (b) for any reference to the Council there were substituted, as respects anything falling to be done on or after the appointed day, a reference to the Secretary of State.

(2) Other documents, not being enactments, which refer to the Council shall be construed in accordance with sub-paragraph (1) so far as applicable.

Legal remedies and pending proceedings

6.—(1) Where any right, liability or obligation is transferred to the Secretary of State by virtue of section 15(1)(b) or paragraph

4(2)(*b*), he and all other persons have the same rights, powers and remedies (and, in particular, the same rights as to the taking or resisting of legal proceedings) for ascertaining, perfecting or enforcing that right, liability or obligation as they would have had if it had at all times been a right, liability or obligation of the Secretary of State.

(2) Any pending legal proceedings by or against the Council which relate to any property, right, liability or obligation transferred to the Secretary of State by virtue of section 15(1)(*b*) or paragraph 4(2)(*b*) may be continued by or against the Secretary of State.

(3) Any reference in sub-paragraph (1) or (2) to legal proceedings shall be construed as including a reference to any application to an authority, and any reference to the taking or resisting of legal proceedings shall be construed accordingly.

Compensation for loss of office

7. If it appears to the Secretary of State that a person who ceases to hold office as a member of the Council on the Council ceasing to exist should receive compensation for loss of office, he may pay that person such sum as, with the approval of the Minister for the Civil Service, he may determine.

Compensation for loss of employment

8.—(1) The Council shall, if they have not done so before the passing of this Act, make a scheme (referred to in this paragraph as the " compensation scheme ") for the payment of compensation, whether by way of a lump sum or periodic payments or by a combination of those methods, to or in respect of persons employed by them who suffer loss of employment which is properly attributable to the winding up of the Council.

(2) The compensation scheme must—

    (*a*) provide for the payment of compensation to be at the discretion of the Council ; and

    (*b*) include provision for an appeal body to determine questions arising.

(3) For the avoidance of doubt, it is declared that the expenses of the Council in making payments under the compensation scheme are administrative expenses of the Council within section 4 of the Harbours Act 1964 (under which such expenses may be funded by charges imposed on harbour authorities), and that the Council's borrowing powers under section 5 of that Act are exercisable for the purpose of making such payments. 1964 c. 40.

(4) As from the appointed day—

    (*a*) the administration of the compensation scheme is the responsibility of the Secretary of State, subject to any direction under sub-paragraph (5) ; and

    (*b*) the expenses of administering the scheme and of making payments under it shall be defrayed by the Secretary of State.

(5) The Secretary of State may direct that the compensation scheme be administered by such person as may be specified in the direction ; and a direction under this sub-paragraph may be revoked or varied by the Secretary of State by a further direction under this sub-paragraph.

(6) The Secretary of State may make such amendments to the compensation scheme as appear to him necessary or expedient in consequence of the winding up of the Council or of the transfer of the administration of the scheme under or by virtue of this paragraph.

Pensions

9.—(1) In this paragraph—

    (a) " the pension scheme " means the National Ports Council Pension Scheme ;

    (b) " the pension fund " means any assets held on trust for the purposes of the pension scheme ; and

    (c) " pension rights " includes all forms of right to or eligibility for the present or future payment of a pension, gratuity or other like payment.

(2) Subject to any direction under sub-paragraph (3), the administration of the pension scheme is the responsibility of the Secretary of State as from the appointed day and on that day the pension fund shall vest in him to be held by him for the purposes of the scheme on the same trusts as subsisted immediately before that day.

(3) The Secretary of State may direct—

    (a) that the pension scheme be administered by, and the pension fund vest in, such person as may be specified in the direction ;

    (b) that the payment of any pension payable otherwise than under the pension scheme to a former member of the Council be the responsibility of such person as may be specified in the direction ;

and a direction under this sub-paragraph may be revoked or varied by the Secretary of State by a further direction under this sub-paragraph.

(4) The Secretary of State may make such amendments to the pension scheme as appear to him necessary or expedient in consequence of the winding up of the Council or of the transfer of the administration of the scheme under or by virtue of this paragraph ; but no such amendment shall prejudice any pension rights existing under the scheme immediately before the amendment takes effect.

(5) There shall be defrayed by the Secretary of State—

    (a) any expenses incurred on or after the appointed day in administering or making payments under the pension scheme, so far as those expenses cannot be met from the pension fund ; and

(*b*) any expenses incurred on or after that day in administering   Sᴄʜ. 5
or paying any such pension as is mentioned in sub-para-
graph (3)(*b*).

Transfer to the Secretary of State of certain of the Council's
former functions

10.—(1) In section 30(4) of the Harbours Act 1964 (duty of 1964 c. 40.
authority to supply copy of list of charges) for " the Council " there
is substituted as from the appointed day " the Secretary of State ".

(2) In section 31 of the Harbours Act 1964 (right of objection
to certain charges) as from the appointed day—

(*a*) for " the Council ", wherever occurring, there is substituted
" the Secretary of State ", and where necessary in consequence of that substitution for pronouns and verbs in
the plural there are substituted corresponding pronouns
and verbs in the singular ; and

(*b*) in subsection (13) the words from " and in relation " to the
end are repealed.

(3) Sections 30(4) and 31 of the Harbours Act 1964, and any
enactment applying in relation to inquiries under the said section 31,
have effect as from the appointed day as if anything previously
done by or in relation to the Council (including any direction given
by the Council and in force immediately before that day) had been
done by or in relation to the Secretary of State.

Information for the Secretary of State

11. In section 41 of the Harbours Act 1964 (power to obtain 1964 c. 40.
information and forecasts), and in section 2 of the Harbours (Loans) 1972 c. 16.
Act 1972 (which extends that power), as from the appointed day—

(*a*) for " the Council ", wherever occurring, there is substituted " the Secretary of State " ; and

(*b*) for " their functions ", wherever occurring, there is substituted " his functions " ;

and any notice served by the Council under the said section 41 and
not complied with before the appointed day has effect on and
after that day as if it had been served by the Secretary of State and
as if the information or forecasts required by it were required to be
furnished to him.

Pending proceedings for harbour
reorganisation scheme

12. A harbour reorganisation scheme submitted to the Secretary
of State by the Council under section 18 of the Harbours Act 1964
which is being proceeded with under Schedule 4 to that Act
immediately before the appointed day shall be proceeded with as
from that day—

(*a*) as if it were one proposed to be made by the Secretary of
State under that section and Schedule as amended by
paragraph 6 of Schedule 6 to this Act ; and

(*b*) as if anything done under and in accordance with the provisions applicable to schemes submitted by the Council had been the corresponding thing to be done under and in accordance with the provisions applicable to schemes proposed to be made by the Secretary of State.

Saving for proceedings under Part I of the Docks and Harbours Act 1966

13. The repeal by this Act of the provisions of Part I of the Docks and Harbours Act 1966 (licensing of dock employers) relating to the functions of the Council does not affect the operation of those provisions in relation to any objection or representation made by the Council before the appointed day, but as from that day the Council shall take no further part in proceedings under that Act.

Textual amendments to facilitate repeals

14.—(1) The following amendments (which do not alter the effect but facilitate express repeals in passages referring to the Council) have effect as from the appointed day.

(2) In section 17(1)(*a*), (*b*) and (*g*) of the Harbours Act 1964 and in Parts I, II and VII of Schedule 3 to that Act for " the Minister ", wherever occurring, there is substituted " the Secretary of State ".

(3) In section 17(1) of the Harbours Act 1964, at the end of the paragraphs there is inserted—

" and the said Parts I, II and VII shall have effect with respect to the procedure for the making of orders by the Minister of Agriculture, Fisheries and Food with the substitution, except in paragraph 6(2), of references to him for references to the Secretary of State."

(4) In paragraph 4(5) and paragraph 8(4) of Schedule 3 to the Harbours Act 1964, and in paragraph 3(6) of Schedule 4 to that Act, for the opening words down to " reported on and " (which require the Secretary of State, before making an order or confirming a scheme, to consider a report of the Council and the documents reported on) there is in each case substituted—

" After considering the objections (if any) made and not withdrawn, and the reports of any person who held an inquiry and any person appointed for the purpose of hearing an objector, the Secretary of State ".

(5) In paragraph 2(*d*) of Schedule 4 to the Harbours Act 1964 for " such a local lighthouse authority as aforesaid " there is substituted " a local lighthouse authority who are not a harbour authority ", and for " the like documents as would be required to be served in compliance with sub-paragraph (*c*) above had the scheme been submitted by the Council " there is substituted " a copy of the scheme, together (if copies of a map or maps were deposited with it) with a copy of that map, or copies of those maps, and, in any event, with a notice stating that the scheme has been submitted to the Secretary of State and that, if the authority served desire to make

to the Secretary of State objection to the scheme, they should do so in writing (stating the grounds of their objection) before the expiration of the period of forty-two days from the date on which the notice is served on them ".

(6) In section 2(5) of the Dock Work Regulation Act 1976 for 1976 c. 79. " others appearing " there is substituted " such persons and bodies as appear ".

Power to adjust local enactments

15.—(1) If it appears to the Secretary of State that the operation of section 15(1)(*a*) or of any of the preceding paragraphs of this Schedule in relation to any enactment of local application (including any provision of a public general Act as applied by such an enactment) is uncertain or produces a result which is anomalous or confusing, he may by order direct that the enactment shall have effect as may be specified in the order, or not have effect, as may appear to him requisite in consequence of section 15 and this Schedule.

(2) An order under this paragraph shall have effect from such date as may be specified in the order, which may be a date before the making of the order but not earlier than the appointed day.

(3) An order under this paragraph shall be made by statutory instrument which shall be subject to annulment in pursuance of a resolution of either House of Parliament.

PART II

FURTHER PROVISIONS WITH RESPECT TO CHARGING SCHEMES

Preliminary

16. In the following provisions of this Schedule " charging scheme " and " harbour authority " have the same meaning as in section 17.

Procedure for making charging scheme

17.—(1) Before he makes a charging scheme the Secretary of State shall publish in such manner as he thinks fit a notice—

(*a*) stating that he proposes to make the scheme ;

(*b*) specifying a place where copies of the draft scheme may be obtained free of charge by harbour authorities affected by the scheme ; and

(*c*) stating that a harbour authority who desire to make to the Secretary of State objections to the scheme should do so in writing before the expiration of such period from the date of publication of the notice (not being less than 42 days) as may be specified in the notice,

and shall send a copy of the scheme to each harbour authority known to him whom he believes to be affected by the scheme.

(2) The Secretary of State shall consider any objections duly made to him with respect to the draft scheme and may, if he thinks fit to

Sch. 5   do so, make the scheme either without modification or with such modifications as he thinks fit (but not including any that in any way increase the charges proposed in the draft scheme).

(3) A charging scheme shall come into operation on such date as may be specified in the scheme.

Supplementary and incidental provisions

18. A charging scheme may include such supplementary and incidental provisions as appear to the Secretary of State to be necessary or expedient.

Information

19.—(1) Without prejudice to the generality of paragraph 18, a charging scheme may provide for requiring a harbour authority to whom the scheme relates to furnish to the Secretary of State, and if so required to verify, such information as he may require for the purposes of the scheme, being information relating to—

1964 c. 40.

(a) any harbour (within the meaning of the Harbours Act 1964) which that harbour authority are engaged in improving, maintaining or managing; or

(b) any activities carried on by them at such a harbour; or

(c) any property used by them for the purpose of such a harbour,

and may provide that failure to comply with any such requirement is an offence punishable on summary conviction with a fine not exceeding such sum (not greater than £500) as may be specified in the scheme.

(2) No person shall disclose any information furnished to him in pursuance of a requirement imposed under sub-paragraph (1) except—

(a) with the consent of the person by whom it was furnished; or

(b) in the form of a summary of information so framed as not to enable particulars relating to the businesses of individual persons to be ascertained from it; or

(c) for the purpose of enabling the Secretary of State to discharge his functions under this Part; or

(d) for the purposes of any legal proceedings.

(3) It is an offence for a person—

(a) to make in response to a requirement imposed under sub-paragraph (1) a statement which is false in a material particular and which he knows to be so false;

(b) to disclose any information in contravention of sub-paragraph (2).

(4) An offence under sub-paragraph (3) is punishable—

(*a*) on summary conviction with imprisonment for a term not exceeding six months, or a fine not exceeding the prescribed sum (within the meaning of section 32 of the 1980 c. 43. Magistrates' Courts Act 1980 or section 289B of the Criminal Procedure (Scotland) Act 1975), or both ; 1975 c. 21.

(*b*) on conviction on indictment, with imprisonment for a term not exceeding two years, or a fine, or both.

Repayments and avoidance of over-payments

20. If it appears to the Secretary of State that the contributions paid or to be paid under charging schemes made by him exceed or are likely to exceed the amount necessary for the purpose mentioned in section 16(1), he shall by order made by statutory instrument make such provision as appears to him necessary or expedient for—

(*a*) terminating or reducing liabilities imposed by virtue of those schemes ; or

(*b*) entitling authorities who have paid contributions imposed by virtue of those schemes to repayment of such proportion of those charges as may be determined by the Secretary of State ;

and such an order may contain such supplementary and incidental provisions as appear to the Secretary of State to be necessary or expedient, including provision for modifying so much of any of those schemes as relates to the manner of payment of contributions payable under the scheme.

SCHEDULE 6   Section 18.

Aᴍᴇɴᴅᴍᴇɴᴛs ᴏꜰ ᴛʜᴇ Hᴀʀʙᴏᴜʀs Aᴄᴛ 1964   1964 c. 40.

Abolition of power to make certain grants for harbour works, etc.

1. Section 12 (power to give assistance to harbour authorities by way of grant for harbour works, etc.) is repealed.

Consolidation, etc. of local enactments by harbour revision orders

2. In section 14 (harbour revision orders) after subsection (2) there is inserted—

"(2A) The objects for achieving all or any of which a harbour revision order may be made in relation to a harbour include repealing superseded, obsolete or otherwise unnecessary statutory provisions of local application affecting the harbour, or consolidating any statutory provisions of local application affecting the harbour ; and subsection (2)(*b*) of this section does not apply to an order in so far as it is made for objects mentioned in this subsection.".

*Ancillary provisions in harbour revision and
empowerment orders and harbour reorganisation schemes*

3. In sections 14(3), 16(6) and 18(2)(*i*) (ancillary provisions which
may be included in a harbour revision or empowerment order or in
a harbour reorganisation scheme) for " consequential or incidental "
there is substituted " supplementary, consequential or incidental ".

*Harbour revision and empowerment orders not subject to special
parliamentary procedure in certain cases*

4.—(1) Sections 14(6) and 16(8) (which make all harbour revision
and empowerment orders subject to special parliamentary procedure)
are repealed ; but Schedule 3 is amended as follows.

(2) In Part I of that Schedule (procedure for the making of orders
on application to the Secretary of State), after paragraph 4 there
is inserted—

" 4A.—(1) The provisions of this paragraph have effect where
the Secretary of State makes—

  (*a*) a harbour revision order relating to a harbour in
England or Wales ; or

  (*b*) a harbour empowerment order relating to a harbour or
to works to be carried out in England or Wales,

and, in either case, the order is opposed.

(2) For the purposes of this paragraph an order is opposed
if—

  (*a*) an objection to the application for the order has been
duly made and not withdrawn, not being an objection
which the Secretary of State is entitled to disregard for
the purposes of paragraph 4 above or which in his
opinion is frivolous or trivial ; or

  (*b*) a comment in writing on proposed modifications to
the order applied for has been duly made to the
Secretary of State and not withdrawn, which in his
opinion would if duly raised in connection with a
provision of the original draft order have amounted
to such an objection as is mentioned in paragraph
(*a*) above ;

and references in this paragraph to a person opposing the order
shall be construed accordingly.

(3) The Secretary of State shall give notice of the making of
the order and its effect to each person opposing the order and
the order shall, subject to sub-paragraph (4) below, become
operative on the expiration of 28 days from the date of the notice
given (or last given) under this sub-paragraph or on such later
date as the Secretary of State may appoint.

(4) If within 28 days after the date of a notice given to him
under sub-paragraph (3) above a person gives notice to the
Secretary of State that he maintains his opposition to the order,
and his opposition is not withdrawn within that period, the
order shall be subject to special parliamentary procedure.

4B. A harbour revision order relating to a harbour in Scotland and a harbour empowerment order relating to a harbour or to works to be carried out in Scotland shall in every case be subject to special parliamentary procedure.".

(3) In paragraph 5 (duties of applicant after making of order), at the end of sub-paragraph (*a*) (duty to publish notices) there is inserted " and further stating, in the case of an order to which paragraph 4B above does not apply, whether the order is affected by the provisions of paragraph 4A above and, where it is not so affected, the date on which it came or will come into operation ".

(4) After paragraph 5 there is inserted—

" 5A. Where an order is affected by the provisions of paragraph 4A above but is not, in the event, subject to special parliamentary procedure, the Secretary of State shall as soon as may be after the expiration of the period (or latest period) of 28 days referred to in sub-paragraph (3) of that paragraph publish by Gazette and local advertisement a notice stating that the order is not so subject and indicating the date on which it came or will come into operation.".

(5) In Part II of that Schedule (procedure for the making of orders by the Secretary of State of his own motion), after paragraph 8 there is inserted—

" 8A.—(1) The provisions of this paragraph have effect where the Secretary of State makes—

(*a*) a harbour revision order relating to a harbour in England or Wales ; or

(*b*) a harbour empowerment order relating to a harbour or to works to be carried out in England or Wales,

and, in either case, the order is opposed.

(2) For the purposes of this paragraph an order is opposed if—

(*a*) an objection to the application for the order has been duly made and not withdrawn, not being an objection which the Secretary of State is entitled to disregard for the purposes of paragraph 8 above or which in his opinion is frivolous or trivial ; or

(*b*) a comment in writing on proposed modifications to the order applied for has been duly made to the Secretary of State and not withdrawn, which in his opinion would if duly raised in connection with a provision of the original draft order have amounted to such an objection as is mentioned in paragraph (*a*) above ;

and references in this paragraph to a person opposing the order shall be construed accordingly.

(3) The Secretary of State shall give notice of the making of the order and its effect to each person opposing the order and the order shall, subject to sub-paragraph (4) below, become

C

SCH. 6   operative on the expiration of 28 days from the date of the
notice given (or last given) under this sub-paragraph or on such
later date as the Secretary of State may appoint.

(4) If within 28 days after the date of a notice given to him
under sub-paragraph (3) above a person gives notice to the
Secretary of State that he maintains his opposition to the order,
and his opposition is not withdrawn within that period, the
order shall be subject to special parliamentary procedure.

8B. A harbour revision order relating to a harbour in Scotland and a harbour empowerment order relating to a harbour
or to works to be carried out in Scotland shall in every case be
subject to special parliamentary procedure.".

(6) In paragraph 9 (duty of Secretary of State to publish notice of
making of order, etc.), after " hours " there is inserted " and further
stating, in the case of an order to which paragraph 8B above does
not apply, whether the order is affected by the provisions of
paragraph 8A above and, where it is not so affected, the date on
which it came or will come into operation ".

(7) After paragraph 9 there is inserted—

" 9A. Where an order is affected by the provisions of paragraph 8A above but is not, in the event, subject to special parliamentary procedure, the Secretary of State shall as soon as may
be after the expiration of the period (or latest period) of 28 days
referred to in sub-paragraph (3) of that paragraph publish by
Gazette and local advertisement a notice stating that the order
is not so subject and indicating the date on which it came or will
come into operation.".

(8) The preceding provisions of this paragraph do not apply to a
harbour revision or empowerment order in relation to which the
notices required by paragraph 3(*a*) or 7(*a*) of Schedule 3 have been
published before this paragraph comes into force.

Power to reduce Ministerial appointments to harbour authorities

5.—(1) The following section is inserted after section 15—

" Ministers'   15A.—(1) Each of the Ministers may, subject to sub-
powers to   section (2) of this section, by order vary the constitu-
make orders
about port   tion of a harbour authority so far as it provides for the
appoint-   appointment by him of any member or members of the
ments.   authority—

   (*a*) so as to abolish the power of appointment (ex-
        cept where the power is to appoint the chairman
        of the authority) ; or

   (*b*) so as to provide for the power of appointment
        to be exercised by such other person or persons
        as may be specified in the order.

(2) No order under this section may be made by the
Secretary of State with respect to the constitution of a
harbour authority if under the constitution all the members
of the authority, apart from *ex officio* and co-opted
members, are appointed by him.

(3) An order under this section—

  (*a*) may relate to more than one harbour authority ; and

  (*b*) may contain such supplementary, incidental and consequential provisions as appear to the Minister making the order to be necessary or expedient ;

and where the constitution of a harbour authority provides for the appointment by the Minister making the order of more than one member, an order under this section may make different provision for each member falling to be so appointed and may make provision for some only of those members.

(4) A Minister proposing to make an order under this section shall before doing so consult the harbour authority concerned and such other persons affected, or bodies representative of such persons, as he thinks fit.

(5) In this section " the Ministers " means the Secretary of State and the Minister of Agriculture, Fisheries and Food.".

(2) In section 44 (which provides for a statutory application for review of certain orders within a six week time limit)—

  (*a*) in subsection (1) after " of that Act) " there is inserted, " or an order under section 15A of this Act," ; and

  (*b*) in subsection (3) after "empowerment order " there is inserted ", or an order under section 15A of this Act,".

(3) In section 54(2) (which provides for negative resolution procedure for certain orders) after " 9(1)," there is inserted " 15A,".

Secretary of State's power to make harbour reorganisation schemes of his own motion

6.—(1) In section 18 (harbour reorganisation schemes) the following subsection is inserted after subsection (1) (submission of scheme to Secretary of State by relevant authorities)—

  " (1A) If the Secretary of State is of opinion that, with a view to securing the efficient and economical development of any such group of harbours as is mentioned in subsection (1) of this section, a harbour reorganisation scheme ought to be made providing for all or any of the matters for which provision may be made by such a scheme, he may by order make a harbour reorganisation scheme providing for those matters.".

(2) For subsection (4) of section 18 (which introduces Schedule 4 and provides for special parliamentary procedure) there is substituted—

  " (4) The provisions of Schedule 4 to this Act shall have effect as follows with respect to the procedure for confirming and making harbour reorganisation schemes—

    (*a*) Part I of that Schedule shall have effect with respect to the procedure for confirming schemes submitted to the Secretary of State ;

(*b*) Part 1 of that Schedule shall, subject to the modifications specified in Part II thereof, have effect with respect to the procedure for the making of schemes by the Secretary of State of his own motion ;

and a harbour reorganisation scheme as confirmed or made by the Secretary of State shall be subject to special parliamentary procedure.".

(3) In subsections (5) and (6) of section 18 (restrictions on orders containing certain provisions) after " confirm " there is inserted " or make ".

(4) In section 44 (statutory application for review of orders within six week time limit), in subsection (4) (which extends the foregoing provisions of the section to harbour reorganisation schemes)—

(*a*) after " confirmed ", where first occurring, there is inserted " or made " ; and

(*b*) after "with the substitution" there is inserted ", in relation to a harbour reorganisation scheme confirmed by the Secretary of State,".

(5) In section 47(3) (inquiries into schemes relating to Scotland) after " confirmation " there is inserted " or making ".

(6) For the heading before paragraph 1 of Schedule 4 there is substituted—

" PROCEDURE FOR CONFIRMING AND MAKING HARBOUR REORGANISATION SCHEMES

PART I

PROCEDURE FOR SUBMISSION AND CONFIRMATION OF HARBOUR REORGANISATION SCHEMES ".

(7) After paragraph 4 of Schedule 4 there is inserted—

" PART II

MODIFICATIONS SUBJECT TO WHICH PART I HAS EFFECT WITH RESPECT TO PROCEDURE FOR MAKING OF HARBOUR REORGANISATION SCHEMES BY THE SECRETARY OF STATE OF HIS OWN MOTION.

5. References to confirming a scheme shall be construed as references to making a scheme.

6. Paragraph 1 shall be omitted.

7. In paragraph 2—

(*a*) for the opening words down to " proceed " there shall be substituted " Where the Secretary of State proposes to make, of his own motion, a harbour reorganisation scheme " ;

(*b*) for the words " has been submitted to " wherever occurring there shall be substituted the words " is proposed to be made by " and in sub-paragraph (*d*) the words " and are not parties to the submission of the scheme " shall be omitted ;

(*c*) for any reference in sub-paragraph (*a*), (*b*) or (*d*) to a map deposited with the scheme there shall be substituted a reference to a map to be annexed to the scheme.

8. In paragraph 3—

    (*a*) in sub-paragraph (1) for the words "submitted to" there shall be substituted the words "proposed to be made by";

    (*b*) in sub-paragraph (7) for the words "as submitted to him" there shall be substituted the words "as served under paragraph 2(*d*) above on the authorities there mentioned", and there shall be omitted the words "that submitted the scheme to him" and the words "that submitted the scheme".

9. In paragraph 4 for the words "submitted to" there shall be substituted the words "proposed to be made by".".

(8) In section 42(2) of the Docks and Harbours Act 1966 (further provision as to harbour reorganisation schemes)— 1966 c. 28.

    (*a*) for "submission and confirmation" there is substituted "confirmation and making"; and

    (*b*) in paragraph (*b*), for the words from "a submission" to "in relation to" there is substituted "the submission to the Secretary of State of a harbour reorganisation scheme and to a proposal by the Secretary of State to make such a scheme of his own motion as it applies in relation to the making of".

Abolition of power to make control of movement orders

7. Sections 20 to 25 and Schedule 5 (control of movement orders) are repealed.

Ship, passenger and goods dues and other charges

8.—(1) After section 27 there is inserted—

"Combined charges.

    27A.—(1) Where a harbour authority have power, whether by virtue of section 26 of this Act or any other statutory provision—

        (*a*) to levy ship, passenger and goods dues or equivalent dues; and

        (*b*) to make other charges,

the authority may, subject to the next following subsection, make a combined charge, that is to say, a single charge referable in part to matters for which ship, passenger and goods dues or equivalent dues may be levied and in part to matters for which other charges may be made.

    (2) A harbour authority may not make a combined charge in any case where—

        (*a*) the person who would be liable to pay the charge objects to paying a combined charge; or

D

>   (*b*) a number of persons would be jointly and
>   severally liable to pay the charge and any of
>   them objects to paying a combined charge :
> but without prejudice to the power of the authority to
> make separate charges in such a case.

(3) A person may not object under subection (2) above
to the payment of a combined charge previously incurred or incurred in pursuance of a prior agreement
between that person and the harbour authority.

(4) In this section " equivalent dues " means dues
exigible in respect of things other than ships for entering,
using or leaving a harbour, including charges for marking
or lighting the harbour.".

(2) In section 30 (duties with respect to keeping of lists of charges,
etc.) after subsection (4) there is inserted—

" (5) Subsection (1) of this section does not apply to combined
charges within the meaning of section 27A of this Act.

(6) References in this section to the dues or charges exigible
by an authority or Board are references to the amount exigible
where no composition agreement applies and no specially agreed
rebate is allowed.".

(3) In section 31 (right of objection to ship, passenger and goods
dues), at the end of subsection (1) (charges to which the section
applies) there is inserted " other than combined charges within the
meaning of section 27A of this Act ; and references in this section
to the rate at which any such charge is imposed are to the amount
where no composition agreement applies and no specially agreed
rebate is allowed ".

Abolition of power to revise certain charges

9.—(1) Sections 32 to 34 (powers of Ministers to revise ship,
passenger and goods dues) are repealed.

(2) Section 35 (local light dues) is repealed so far as it applies
sections 32 and 34.

Accounts and reports relating to harbour activities and
associated activities

10. For section 42 (accounts relating to harbour undertakings)
there is substituted—

" Accounts
and reports
relating
to harbour
activities
and
associated
activities.

42.—(1) It shall be the duty of every statutory harbour
undertaker to prepare an annual statement of accounts
relating to the harbour activities and to any associated
activities carried on by him.

(2) Where a statutory harbour undertaker is a holding
company with subsidiaries which carry on harbour
activities or any associated activities, then, without
prejudice to the company's duty under subsection (1)
above, it shall be the duty of the company to prepare
an annual statement of accounts relating to the harbour
activities and associated activities carried on by it and
its subsidiaries.

(3) The requirements of subsection (1) or subsection (2) above are not satisfied by the preparation of a statement of accounts which relates to other matters in addition to harbour activities and associated activities.

(4) Where provision is made for the auditing of accounts prepared by any person otherwise than under this section which relate to harbour activities carried on by him (whether or not they relate to other matters) that provision shall apply also to any statement prepared by him under this section.

(5) It shall be the duty of any person by whom a statement of accounts is prepared in accordance with this section—

   (a) to send to the Secretary of State a copy of the statement together with a copy of the auditor's report on it ; and

   (b) to prepare and send to the Secretary of State a report on the state of affairs disclosed by the statement.

(6) Subject to any regulations made under the next following subsection, the provisions of the Companies Acts 1948 to 1980 as to the form and contents of accounts and reports required to be prepared under those Acts shall apply to accounts and reports required to be prepared under this section, as follows—

   (a) the provisions relating to company accounts shall apply to statements prepared in accordance with subsection (1) above ;

   (b) the provisions relating to group accounts shall apply to statements prepared in accordance with subsection (2) above ; and

   (c) the provisions relating to the directors' report required to be attached to a company's balance sheet shall apply to reports prepared in accordance with subsection (5)(b) above.

(7) The Secretary of State may make provision by regulations with respect to the form and contents of accounts and reports prepared under this section—

   (a) prescribing cases in which the provisions of the Companies Acts 1948 to 1980 referred to in subsection (6) above are not to apply ;

   (b) modifying those provisions ;

   (c) prescribing requirements additional to those imposed by those provisions.

(8) Where a statutory harbour undertaker is obliged by a statutory provision of local application to prepare accounts, then, so far as those accounts relate to harbour activities or associated activities, any requirements of the

statutory provision of local application as to the form and contents of the accounts shall be treated as satisfied by the preparation of accounts in the same manner that is required for a statement under this section.

(9) In this section—

"associated activities", in relation to any harbour activities means such activities as may be prescribed in relation to those activities by regulations made by the Secretary of State;

"harbour activities" means activities involved in carrying on a statutory harbour undertaking or in carrying out harbour operations;

"holding company" and "subsidiary" have the meaning given by section 154 of the Companies Act 1948;

"statutory harbour undertaking" means an undertaking, or part of an undertaking, whose activities consist wholly or mainly of the improvement, maintenance or management of a harbour in the exercise and performance of statutory powers and duties, and "statutory harbour undertaker" shall be construed accordingly.

(10) Regulations under subsection (7) or (9) above may be made so as to apply to all undertakers, to a class of undertakers or to a particular undertaker.

(11) This section does not apply to—

(*a*) the Boards;

(*b*) a statutory harbour undertaker the activities of whose undertaking consist wholly or mainly in the improvement, maintenance or management of a fishery harbour or marine work;

(*c*) a statutory harbour undertaker of a class exempted from this section by regulations made by the Secretary of State.".

Inquiries

1972 c. 70.
1964 c. 40.

11.—(1) In section 47(1) (which as amended by section 272(2) of the Local Government Act 1972 applies certain provisions of section 250 of that Act to inquiries and hearings under the Harbours Act 1964), paragraph (*a*)(i) and the words "(i) and" (which are ineffective as a result of that amendment) are repealed.

1936 c. 52.

(2) In section 47(3) (power to direct that inquiries in Scotland be held by Commissioners under the Private Legislation Procedure (Scotland) Act 1936) for "or paragraph 3(3) of Schedule 4" there is substituted "or paragraph 3(5) of Schedule 4".

Abolition of preliminary consideration of application for harbour revision or empowerment order

12. Paragraph 2 of Schedule 3 (Secretary of State's preliminary consideration of applications for harbour revision or empowerment orders) is repealed ; and accordingly in paragraph 3 of that Schedule—

(*a*) for the words from the beginning to " allowed to proceed " there is substituted " Where an application for a harbour revision order has been duly made to the Secretary of State " ;

(*b*) for " further steps " there is substituted " any steps (otherwise than under this paragraph) " ; and

(*c*) in paragraph (*d*) for " be contemporaneously " there is substituted " and within such time as may be so specified, be ".

Penalties for offences

13.—(1) In section 10(3) (obstruction of, or failure to assist, person appointed to inspect books, records and documents) for " £20 " there is substituted " £200 ".

(2) In section 31(8) (failure by authority to comply with direction) for " £100 " there is substituted " £500 ".

(3) In section 41(3) (failure to comply with notice to furnish information or forecasts) for the words from " £50 " to the end there is substituted " £500 ".

(4) The amendments made by this paragraph do not apply in relation to offences committed before this paragraph comes into force.

14.—(1) Sections 14(3) and 16(6) (penalties which may be provided for by harbour revision or empowerment orders or harbour reorganisation schemes) are amended as follows.

(2) In paragraph (*a*) (penalties on summary conviction), for " the infliction on him of a fine exceeding £100 " there is substituted—
" —

(i) in the case of an offence triable either summarily or on indictment, the infliction on him of a fine exceeding the prescribed sum within the meaning of section 32 of the Magistrates' Courts Act 1980 or section 289B of the Criminal Procedure (Scotland) Act 1975 ;

(ii) in the case of an offence triable only summarily, the infliction on him of a fine exceeding £500 or, in the case of a continuing offence, a daily fine exceeding £50 for each day on which the offence continues after conviction ; ".

(3) In paragraph (*b*) (penalties on conviction on indictment) for the words from " imprisonment " to the end there is substituted " a penalty other than a fine "

15.—(1) In sections 45(i) and 46(2)(*a*) (penalties on summary conviction for, respectively, furnishing false information and improperly disclosing information or forecasts) for " three months " there is substituted " six months ".

D 3

(2) The amendments made by this paragraph do not apply in relation to offences committed before this paragraph comes into force.

SCHEDULE 7

PENALTY POINTS

PART I

OFFENCES WHERE DISQUALIFICATION OBLIGATORY
EXCEPT FOR SPECIAL REASONS

Description of offence	Number of penalty points
Any offence involving obligatory disqualification (within the meaning of Part III of Road Traffic Act 1972).	4

PART II

OFFENCES WHERE DISQUALIFICATION DISCRETIONARY

A—Offences under Road Traffic Act 1972

Section of 1972 Act creating offence	Description	Number of penalty points
2 ...	Reckless driving	10
3 ...	Careless or inconsiderate driving	2—5
5(2) ...	Being in charge of motor vehicle when unfit through drink or drugs.	10
6(1)(*b*) ...	Being in charge of motor vehicle with alcohol above prescribed limit.	10
7(4) ...	Failing to provide specimen for breath test ...	4
8(7) ...	Failing to provide specimen for analysis ...	10
16 ...	Carrying passenger on motor cycle contrary to section 16.	1
22 ...	Failing to comply with traffic directions ...	3
24 ...	Leaving vehicle in dangerous position	3
25(4) ...	Failing to stop after accident	5—9
25(4) ...	Failing to give particulars or report accident ...	4—9
40(5) ...	Contravention of construction and use regulations.	3
84(1) ...	Driving without licence	2
88(6) ...	Failing to comply with conditions of licence ...	2
91(1) ...	Driving with uncorrected defective eyesight ...	2
91(2) ...	Refusing to submit to test of eyesight	2
99(*b*) ...	Driving while disqualified as under age ...	2
99(*b*) ...	Driving while disqualified by order of court ...	6
143 ...	Using, or causing or permitting use of, motor vehicle uninsured and unsecured against third-party risks.	4—8
175 ...	Taking in Scotland a motor vehicle without consent or lawful authority or driving, or allowing oneself to be carried in, a motor vehicle so taken.	8

B—Offences under other Acts   SCH. 7
(*or, where stated, attempts*)

Act and section creating offence or providing for its punishment	Description	Number of penalty points
Road Traffic Regulation Act 1967 s. 13(4).	Contravention of traffic regulations on special roads.	3
Road Traffic Regulation Act 1967 s. 23(5).	Contravention of pedestrian crossing regulations.	3
Road Traffic Regulation Act 1967 s. 25(2).	Failure to obey sign exhibited by school crossing patrol.	3
Road Traffic Regulation Act 1967 s. 26(6), s. 26A(5).	Contravention of order prohibiting or restricting use of street playground by vehicles.	2
Road Traffic Regulation Act 1967 s. 78A.	Exceeding a speed limit	3
Theft Act 1968 s. 12 ...	Taking or attempting to take conveyance without consent or lawful authority or driving or attempting to drive a motor vehicle so taken or allowing oneself to be carried in a motor vehicle so taken.	8
Theft Act 1968 s. 25 ...	Going equipped for stealing with reference to theft or taking of motor vehicle.	8

C—Thefts and attempted thefts

Description of offence	Number of penalty points
Stealing or attempting to steal motor vehicle ...	8

Note: The descriptions of offences under A and B above indicate only their general nature.

SCHEDULE 8   Section 25.

PROVISIONS SUBSTITUTED FOR SECTIONS 6 TO 12 OF THE ROAD TRAFFIC ACT 1972

Driving or being in charge of a motor vehicle with alcohol concentration above prescribed limit.

6.—(1) If a person—

(*a*) drives or attempts to drive a motor vehicle on a road or other public place ; or

(*b*) is in charge of a motor vehicle on a road or other public place ;

after consuming so much alcohol that the proportion of it in his breath, blood or urine exceeds the prescribed limit he shall be guilty of an offence.

(2) It is a defence for a person charged with an offence under subsection (1)(*b*) above to prove that at the time

D 4

SCH. 8

he is alleged to have committed the offence the circumstances were such that there was no likelihood of his driving the vehicle whilst the proportion of alcohol in his breath, blood or urine remained likely to exceed the prescribed limit; but in determining whether there was such a likelihood the court may disregard any injury to him and any damage to the vehicle.

Breath tests.

7.—(1) Where a constable in uniform has reasonable cause to suspect—

(a) that a person driving or attempting to drive or in charge of a motor vehicle on a road or other public place has alcohol in his body or has committed a traffic offence whilst the vehicle was in motion; or

(b) that a person has been driving or attempting to drive or been in charge of a motor vehicle on a road or other public place with alcohol in his body and that that person still has alcohol in his body; or

(c) that a person has been driving or attempting to drive or been in charge of a motor vehicle on a road or other public place and has committed a traffic offence whilst the vehicle was in motion;

he may, subject to section 9 below, require him to provide a specimen of breath for a breath test.

(2) If an accident occurs owing to the presence of a motor vehicle on a road or other public place a constable may require any person who he has reasonable cause to believe was driving or attempting to drive or in charge of the vehicle at the time of the accident to provide a specimen of breath for a breath test, but subject to section 9 below.

(3) A person may be required under subsection (1) or subsection (2) of this section to provide a specimen either at or near the place where the requirement is made or, if the requirement is made under subsection (2) and the constable making the requirement thinks fit, at a police station specified by the constable.

(4) A person who, without reasonable excuse, fails to provide a specimen of breath when required to do so in pursuance of this section shall be guilty of an offence.

(5) A constable may arrest a person without warrant if—

(a) as a result of a breath test he has reasonable cause to suspect that the proportion of alcohol in that person's breath or blood exceeds the prescribed limit; or

(b) that person has failed to provide a specimen of breath for a breath test when required to do so in pursuance of this section and the constable has reasonable cause to suspect that he has alcohol in his body;

but a person shall not be arrested by virtue of this sub-   Sch. 8
section when he is at a hospital as a patient.

(6) For the purpose of requiring a person to provide
a specimen of breath under subsection (2) above in a
case where he has reasonable cause to suspect that the
accident involved injury to another person or of arresting him in such a case under subsection (5) above a
constable may enter (if need be by force) any place
where that person is or where the constable, with reasonable cause, suspects him to be.

(7) Subsection (6) above does not extend to Scotland
and nothing in that subsection shall affect any rule of
law in Scotland concerning the right of a constable to
enter any premises for any purpose.

(8) In this section " traffic offence " means an offence
under any provision of this Act except Part V, or under
any provision of Part III of the Road Traffic Act 1960, 1960 c. 16.
the Road Traffic Regulation Act 1967 or Part I of the 1967 c. 76.
Transport Act 1980. 1980 c. 34.

Provision of   **8.**—(1) In the course of an investigation whether a
specimens   person has committed an offence under section 5 or
for analysis.   section 6 of this Act a constable may, subject to the
following provisions of this section and section 9 below,
require him—

    (*a*) to provide two specimens of breath for analysis
by means of a device of a type approved by the
Secretary of State ; or

    (*b*) to provide a specimen of blood or urine for a
laboratory test.

(2) A requirement under this section to provide specimens of breath can only be made at a police station.

(3) A requirement under this section to provide a
specimen of blood or urine can only be made at a police
station or at a hospital ; and it cannot be made at a
police station unless—

    (*a*) the constable making the requirement has rea-
sonable cause to believe that for medical reasons
a specimen of breath cannot be provided or
should not be required ; or

    (*b*) at the time the requirement is made a device or
a reliable device of the type mentioned in subsection (1)(*a*) is not available at the police
station or it is then for any other reason not
practicable to use such a device there ; or

    (*c*) the suspected offence is one under section 5 of
this Act and the constable making the requirement has been advised by a medical practitioner
that the condition of the person required to
provide the specimen might be due to some
drug ;

but may then be made notwithstanding that the person required to provide the specimen has already provided or been required to provide two specimens of breath.

(4) If the provision of a specimen other than a specimen of breath may be required in pursuance of this section the question whether it is to be a specimen of blood or a specimen of urine shall be decided by the constable making the requirement, except that if a medical practitioner is of the opinion that for medical reasons a specimen of blood cannot or should not be taken the specimen shall be a specimen of urine.

(5) A specimen of urine shall be provided within one hour of the requirement for its provision being made and after the provision of a previous specimen of urine.

(6) Of any two specimens of breath provided by any person in pursuance of this section that with the lower proportion of alcohol in the breath shall be used and the other shall be disregarded; but if the specimen with the lower proportion of alcohol contains no more than 50 microgrammes of alcohol in 100 millilitres of breath the person who provided it may claim that it should be replaced by such a specimen as may be required under subsection (4), and if he then provides such a specimen neither specimen of breath shall be used.

(7) A person who, without reasonable excuse, fails to provide a specimen when required to do so in pursuance of this section shall be guilty of an offence.

(8) On requiring any person to provide a specimen in pursuance of this section a constable shall warn him that a failure to provide it may render him liable to prosecution.

(9) The Secretary of State may by regulations substitute another proportion of alcohol in the breath for that specified in subsection (6).

Protection for hospital patients.

9.—(1) While a person is at a hospital as a patient he shall not be required to provide a specimen of breath for a breath test or to provide a specimen for a laboratory test unless the medical practitioner in immediate charge of his case has been notified of the proposal to make the requirement; and—

(a) if the requirement is then made it shall be for the provision of a specimen at the hospital; but

(b) if the medical practitioner objects on the ground specified in subsection (2) below the requirement shall not be made.

(2) The ground on which the medical practitioner may object is that the requirement or the provision of a specimen or, in the case of a specimen of blood or urine, the warning required under section 8(8) above, would be prejudicial to the proper care and treatment of the patient.

Evidence in
proceedings
for an
offence
under s. 5
or s. 6.

SCH. 8

10.—(1) The following provisions apply with respect to proceedings for an offence under section 5 or section 6 of this Act.

(2) Evidence of the proportion of alcohol or any drug in a specimen of breath, blood or urine provided by the accused shall, in all cases, be taken into account, and it shall be assumed that the proportion of alcohol in the accused's breath, blood or urine at the time of the alleged offence was not less than in the specimen; but if the proceedings are for an offence under section 6 of this Act, or for an offence under section 5 of this Act in a case where the accused is alleged to have been unfit through drink, the assumption shall not be made if the accused proves—

   (a) that he consumed alcohol after he had ceased to drive, attempt to drive or be in charge of a motor vehicle on a road or other public place and before he provided the specimen; and

   (b) that had he not done so the proportion of alcohol in his breath, blood or urine would not have exceeded the prescribed limit and, if the proceedings are for an offence under section 5 of this Act, would not have been such as to impair his ability to drive properly.

(3) Evidence of the proportion of alcohol or a drug in a specimen of breath, blood or urine may, subject to subsections (5) and (6) below, be given by the production of a document or documents purporting to be whichever of the following is appropriate, that is to say—

   (a) a statement automatically produced by the device by which the proportion of alcohol in a specimen of breath was measured and a certificate signed by a constable (which may but need not be contained in the same document as the statement) that the statement relates to a specimen provided by the accused at the date and time shown in the statement; and

   (b) a certificate signed by an authorised analyst as to the proportion of alcohol or any drug found in a specimen of blood or urine identified in the certificate.

(4) A specimen of blood shall be disregarded unless it was taken from the accused with his consent by a medical practitioner; but evidence that a specimen of blood was so taken may be given by the production of a document purporting to certify that fact and to be signed by a medical practitioner.

(5) A document purporting to be such a statement or such a certificate, or both such a statement and such a certificate, as is mentioned in subsection (3)(a) above is admissible in evidence on behalf of the prosecution in

pursuance of this section only if a copy of it either has been handed to the accused when the document was produced or has been served on him not later than seven days before the hearing, and any other document is so admissible only if a copy of it has been served on the accused not later than seven days before the hearing; but a document purporting to be a certificate (or so much of a document as purports to be a certificate) is not so admissible if the accused, not later than three days before the hearing or within such further time as the court may in special circumstances allow, has served notice on the prosecutor requiring the attendance at the hearing of the person by whom the document purports to be signed.

(6) Where, at the time a specimen of blood or urine was provided by the accused, he asked to be supplied with such a specimen, evidence of the proportion of alcohol or any drug found in the specimen is not admissible on behalf of the prosecution unless—

    (*a*) the specimen in which the alcohol or drug was found is one of two parts into which the specimen provided by the accused was divided at the time it was provided; and

    (*b*) the other part was supplied to the accused.

(7) In Scotland—

    (*a*) a document produced in evidence on behalf of the prosecution in pursuance of subsection (3) or (4) above and, where the person by whom the document was signed is called as a witness, the evidence of that person, shall be sufficient evidence of the facts stated in the document; and

    (*b*) a written execution purporting to be signed by the person who handed to or served on the accused or the prosecutor a copy of the document or of the notice in terms of subsection (5) above, together with, where appropriate, a post office receipt for the relative registered or recorded delivery letter shall be sufficient evidence of the handing or service of such a copy or notice.

(8) A copy of a certificate required by this section to be served on the accused or a notice required by this section to be served on the prosecutor may be served personally or sent by registered post or recorded delivery service.

(9) In this section "authorised analyst" means any person possessing the qualifications prescribed by regulations made under section 89 of the Food and Drugs Act 1955 or section 27 of the Food and Drugs (Scotland) Act 1956 as qualifying persons for appointment as public analysts under those Acts, and any other person authorised by the Secretary of State to make analyses for the purposes of this section.

1955 (4 & 5
Eliz. 2.) c. 16.
1956 c. 30.

Detention of persons affected by alcohol or a drug.

11. A person required to provide a specimen of breath, blood or urine may thereafter be detained at a police station until it appears to a constable that, were that person then driving or attempting to drive a motor vehicle on a road, he would not be committing an offence under section 5 or section 6 of this Act ; but—

SCH. 8

> (*a*) a person shall not be detained in pursuance of this section if it appears to a constable that there is no likelihood of his driving or attempting to drive a motor vehicle whilst his ability to drive properly is impaired or whilst the proportion of alcohol in his breath, blood or urine exceeds the prescribed limit ; and
>
> (*b*) a constable shall consult a medical practitioner on any question arising under this section whether a person's ability to drive properly is or might be impaired through drugs and shall act on the medical practitioner's advice.

Interpretation of sections 5 to 11.

12.—(1) The following provisions apply for the interpretation of sections 5 to 11 of this Act.

(2) In those sections—

> " breath test " means a preliminary test for the purpose of obtaining, by means of a device of a type approved by the Secretary of State, an indication whether the proportion of alcohol in a person's breath or blood is likely to exceed the prescribed limit ;
>
> " drug " includes any intoxicant other than alcohol ;
>
> " fail " includes refuse ;
>
> " hospital " means an institution which provides medical or surgical treatment for in-patients or out-patients ;
>
> " the prescribed limit " means, as the case may require—
>
>> (*a*) 35 microgrammes of alcohol in 100 millilitres of breath ;
>>
>> (*b*) 80 milligrammes of alcohol in 100 millilitres of blood ; or
>>
>> (*c*) 107 milligrammes of alcohol in 100 millilitres of urine ;
>>
>> or such other proportion as may be prescribed by regulations made by the Secretary of State.

(3) A person does not provide a specimen of breath for a breath test or for analysis unless the specimen is sufficient to enable the test or the analysis to be carried out.

(4) A person provides a specimen of blood if and only if he consents to its being taken by a medical practitioner and it is so taken.

SCHEDULE 9

CONSEQUENTIAL AND MINOR AMENDMENTS OF ROAD TRAFFIC ACT
1972 AND SECTION 56 OF CRIMINAL JUSTICE ACT 1967

PART I

THE ROAD TRAFFIC ACT 1972

1. In section 13 for " 9 " there is substituted " 8 ".

2. Sections 93(3) and (5) are omitted.

3. In section 93(4) for " 9(3) " there is substituted " 8(7) ".

4. In section 93(7) after the words " under the foregoing provisions
of this section " there are inserted the words " or under section 19 of
the Transport Act 1981 ".

5. In section 94(1) for the words " section 93(1) or (3) of this Act "
there are substituted the words " section 93 of this Act or section 19
of the Transport Act 1981 ".

6. In section 101(1) for the words from " the court shall order " to
the end there are substituted the words " the court shall order that
there shall be endorsed on any licence held by him particulars of the
conviction and, if the court orders him to be disqualified, particulars
of the disqualification, and, if the court does not order him to be
disqualified, the particulars and penalty points required by section
19(1) of the Transport Act 1981 ; and the endorsement may be
produced as prima facie evidence of the matters endorsed.".

7. In section 101(2) for the words from " need not " to " as aforesaid " there are substituted the words " need not make an order under
subsection (1) above ".

8. In section 101(3) for the words from the beginning to " by him "
there are substituted the words " An order that any particulars or
penalty points are to be endorsed on any licence held by the convicted person " and at the end there are added the words " or penalty points ".

9. In section 101(4A) at the end there are added the words " and
any penalty points endorsed on it which are to be taken into
account under section 19(3) of the Transport Act 1981 ".

10. In section 101(5) after the word " particulars ", in both places,
there are added the words " or penalty points ".

11. In section 101(6) after the word " particulars ", in the first and
second places where it occurs, there are added the words " or penalty points ".

12. For section 101(7) there are substituted the following subsections : —

" (7) A person whose licence has been ordered to be endorsed
(whether under this section or a previous enactment) shall be
entitled to have a new licence issued to him free from the
endorsement if, after the end of the period for which the endorsement remains effective, he applies for a new licence in pursuance
of subsection (1) of section 88 of this Act, surrenders any subsisting licence, pays the prescribed fee and satisfies the other
requirements of that subsection.

(7A) An endorsement ordered on a person's conviction of an offence remains effective—

   (a) if an order is made for the disqualification of the offender, until four years have elapsed since the conviction ; and

   (b) if no such order is made, until either four years have elapsed since the commission of the offence or such an order is made ;

but if the offence was one under section 1 or 2 of this Act the endorsement remains in any case effective until four years have elapsed since the conviction, and if it was one under section 5(1) or 6(1)(a) of this Act or was one under section 8(7) of this Act involving obligatory disqualification, the endorsement remains effective until eleven years have elapsed since the conviction.".

13. The words " or section 19 of the Transport Act 1981 " are inserted—

   (a) at the end of section 102(1) ;

   (b) in section 103(1) after the words " section 93 of this Act " ;

   (c) in section 103(3) after the words " section 93 of this Act " ; and

   (d) in section 105(1) after the words " section 93 or 101 of this Act ".

14. For section 105(2) there is substituted the following:

   " (2) Where a court orders the endorsement of any licence held by a person it may, and if the court orders him to be disqualified it shall, send the licence, on its being produced to the court, to the Secretary of State ; and if the court orders the endorsement but does not send the licence to the Secretary of State it shall send him notice of the endorsement.".

15. In section 182(2A)—

   (a) in paragraph (b), after the words " any such offence " there are inserted the words " or any order made on the conviction " ;

   (b) in paragraph (c) and in the words following paragraph (d), after the words " the previous conviction " there are inserted the words " or order ".

16. In section 188(6) for the words from " motor cycles whereof " to " cubic centimetres " there are substituted the words " certain motor cycles ".

17. In subsection (1) of section 189 (application of sections 6 to 11 to persons subject to service discipline)—

   (a) in paragraph (f) for " section 8(1) " there is substituted " section 7(1) " ;

   (b) paragraph (g) is omitted ; and

   (c) in paragraph (h) for " subsection (4) " there is substituted " subsection (7) ".

18. In section 199 (exercise of regulation making powers etc.)—

   (a) in subsection (2) the words " 12(1) or " are omitted ;

   (b) in subsection (3) for " 12(1) " there is substituted " 8(9), 12(2), 33A " ; and

(c) in subsection (4) for " 12(1) " there is substituted " 8(9), 12(2) or 33A ".

19. In Part I of Schedule 4 (prosecution and punishment of offences under 1972 Act) for the words in columns 1 and 2 of the entries relating to section 6(1) and 6(2) there are substituted the words :

" 6(1)(a)   Driving or attempting to drive with excess alcohol in breath, blood or urine. "

and

"6(1)(b)   Being in charge of a motor vehicle with excess alcohol in breath, blood or urine."

20. In Part I of Schedule 4, in the first coloumn of the entry relating to section 8(3), for " 8(3) " there is substituted " 7(4) " and in the fifth and sixth columns of the entry there are inserted respectively " Discretionary " and " Obligatory ".

21. In Part I of Schedule 4, in the entry relating to section 9(3), the following is substituted for the words in columns 1 to 5 : —

8(7) Failing to provide specimen for analysis or laboratory test.	Summarily	(a) Where the specimen was required to ascertain ability to drive or proportion of alcohol at the time offender was driving or attempting to drive, six months or £1,000 or both. (b) In any other case three months or £500 or both.	(a) Obligatory in case mentioned in paragraph (a) of column 4. (b) Discretionary in any other case.

22. In Part I of Schedule 4, in the fifth column of the entry relating to section 22, after the word " constable " there are inserted the words " or traffic warden ".

23. In Part V of Schedule 4, paragraph 1 is omitted.

24. In Schedule 10, in paragraph 5 for " 9(3) " (in both places) there is substituted " 8(7) ".

PART II

SECTION 56 OF THE CRIMINAL JUSTICE ACT 1967 (c. 80)

25. The words " or section 19 of the Transport Act 1981 " are inserted after the words " the Road Traffic Act 1972 " in subsections 1(b), (6) and (13).

SCHEDULE 10

ROAD HUMPS

PART I

PROVISION FOR ENGLAND AND WALES

1. In section 62(3) of the Highways Act (descriptions of works for which specific powers are given and in relation to which the general power in that section does not apply), the following paragraph is inserted after paragraph (f)—

" (f) the construction, maintenance and removal of road humps ; ".

2. The following provisions are inserted after section 90 of the
Highways Act 1980—

" Road humps

Construc-
tion of
road humps
by highway
authority.

90A.—(1) A highway authority may construct road
humps in a highway maintainable at the public expense
for which they are the highway authority if—

> (a) the highway is subject to a statutory speed limit
> for motor vehicles of 30 miles per hour or less ;
> or
>
> (b) the road humps are specially authorised by the
> Secretary of State,

and may remove any road humps so constructed by
them.

(2) The consent of the Greater London Council is
required for the construction of road humps under this
section by a London borough council or the Common
Council.

Additional
powers
of the
Secretary
of State.

90B.—(1) The Secretary of State may construct road
humps in a highway maintainable at the public expense
for which he is not the highway authority if—

> (a) the highway is subject to a statutory speed limit
> for motor vehicles of 30 miles per hour or
> less ; or
>
> (b) the road humps are specially authorised by him,

and may maintain and remove any road humps so constructed by him.

(2) The consent of the local highway authority for the
highway concerned is required for the construction of
road humps under this section and also, in the case of a
highway in Greater London for which the Greater London
Council are not the highway authority, the consent of that
Council.

(3) The Secretary of State and the local highway authority may enter into an agreement for the carrying out
by the local highway authority of any works which the
Secretary of State has power to carry out under this
section.

(4) Subject to subsection (5) below, the consent of the
Secretary of State is required before the local highway
authority or any other person having power to maintain
the highway may remove or otherwise interfere with a
road hump constructed under this section.

(5) If the Secretary of State so directs with the consent
of the local highway authority the local highway authority shall have the same powers in relation to a road
hump constructed under this section as they have in
relation to a road hump constructed by them under section
90A above.

(6) Where a road hump has been constructed under this section, the local highway authority and any other person having power to maintain the highway may reimburse the Secretary of State the whole or part of his expenses in relation to the road hump.

Consultation and local inquiries.

90C.—(1) Where the Secretary of State or a local highway authority propose to construct a road hump under section 90A or 90B above, he or they shall consult with—

(a) the chief officer of police for the area in which the highway concerned is situated ; and

(b) such other persons or bodies as may be prescribed by regulations made by the Secretary of State.

(2) The Secretary of State or local highway authority shall also—

(a) publish in one or more newspapers circulating in the area in which the highway concerned is situated ; and

(b) place at appropriate points on that highway,

a notice of the proposal stating the nature, dimensions and location of the proposed road hump and the address to which and the period within which any objections to the proposal may be sent.

(3) The period stated in a notice under subsection (2) above shall be not less than 21 days beginning with the date on which the notice is first published in accordance with paragraph (a) of that subsection.

(4) The Secretary of State or local highway authority shall consider any objections sent to him or them in accordance with a notice under subsection (2) above and may, if he or they think fit, cause a local inquiry to be held.

(5) Subsections (2) to (5) of section 250 of the Local Government Act 1972 (provisions as to inquiries) have effect in relation to an inquiry held under subsection (4) above as they have effect in relation to an inquiry held under that section, but with such modifications as may be prescribed by regulations made by the Secretary of State.

(6) Before making regulations under this section the Secretary of State shall consult such representative organisations as he thinks fit.

Regulations concerning construction and maintenance of road humps.

90D.—(1) The Secretary of State may by regulations make such provision in relation to the construction and maintenance of road humps as appears to him to be necessary or expedient in the interests of safety and the free movement of traffic, and may in particular—

(a) provide that road humps shall be constructed

only in highways of such descriptions and in such circumstances as may be prescribed by the regulations ;

(*b*) impose requirements as to—

(i) the nature, dimensions, location and spacing of road humps ;

(ii) the placing of signs of such type or character as may be so prescribed ;

(iii) the carrying out and maintenance of other ancillary or consequential works.

(2) Regulations under this section may make different provision for different cases, as for example for road humps and highways of different descriptions.

(3) Before making any regulations under this section the Secretary of State shall consult with such representative organisations as he thinks fit.

(4) Regulations under this section do not apply where a road hump is specially authorised by the Secretary of State, but conditions attached by him to the authorisation may, in particular, relate to any of the matters with respect to which regulations may be made under this section.

Status of road humps.

90E.—(1) Where a road hump conforms to regulations under section 90D above and, in the case of a road hump in a highway maintainable at the public expense, the conditions mentioned in subsection (2) below are satisfied, the road hump shall not be treated as constituting an obstruction to the highway but as part of the highway, so that in particular

(*a*) the obligation of any person to maintain the highway ; and

(*b*) the obligation of any person having power to break open the highway to make good any damage or otherwise reinstate the highway,

extend to maintaining or, as the case may be, making good any damage to or otherwise reinstating the road hump.

(2) The further conditions applicable in the case of a road hump in a highway maintainable at the public expense are—

(*a*) that the highway is for the time being subject to a statutory speed limit for motor vehicles of 30 miles per hour or less or the road hump is specially authorised by the Secretary of State ; and

(*b*) that the road hump was constructed under section 90A or 90B above or was constructed at a time when the highway was not maintainable at the public expense.

SCH. 10.

(3) In relation to a road hump specially authorised by the Secretary of State the reference in subsection (1) above to conformity with regulations shall be construed as a reference to conformity with the conditions attached to the authorisation.

(4) In so far as it does not apply apart from this subsection, Part II of the Public Utilities Street Works Act 1950 (code regulating relations between persons carrying out alterations to roads and statutory undertakers having apparatus in those roads) applies in relation to the construction, maintenance and removal of a road hump as if the works were executed for road purposes and were mentioned in section 21(1)(*a*) of that Act and as if the person executing them were the promoting authority within the meaning of that Part.

Meaning of "road hump" and interpretation of sections 90A to 90E.

90F.—(1) In this Act " road hump " means an artificial hump in or on the surface of the highway which is designed to control the speed of vehicles, and references to a road hump include references to any other works (including signs or lighting) required in connection with such a hump.

(2) In sections 90A to 90E above—

" motor vehicle " has the same meaning as in the Road Traffic Regulation Act 1967 ; and

" statutory " means having effect by virtue of an enactment.".

1980 c. 66.

3. In section 329(1) of the Highways Act 1980 (interpretation) the following is inserted at the appropriate place—

" ' road hump ' has the meaning provided by section 90F(1) ; ".

PART II

PROVISION FOR SCOTLAND

Construction of road humps by highway authority

4. A highway authority may construct road humps in a highway for which they are the highway authority if—

(*a*) the highway is subject to a statutory speed limit for motor vehicles of 30 miles per hour or less ; or

(*b*) the road humps are especially authorised by the Secretary of State,

and may remove any road humps so constructed by them.

Additional powers of the Secretary of State

5.—(1) The Secretary of State may, with the consent of the local highway authority for the highway concerned, construct road humps in a highway for which he is not the highway authority if—

(*a*) the highway is subject to a statutory speed limit for motor vehicles of 30 miles per hour or less : or

(*b*) the road humps are specially authorised by him,
and may maintain and remove any road humps so constructed by
him.

(2) The Secretary of State and the local highway authority may
enter into an agreement for the carrying out by the local highway
authority of any works which the Secretary of State has power to
carry out under this paragraph.

(3) Subject to sub-paragraph (4), the consent of the Secretary of
State is required before the local highway authority may remove or
otherwise interfere with a road hump constructed under this
paragraph.

(4) If the Secretary of State so directs with the consent of the local
highway authority, the local highway authority shall have the same
powers in relation to a road hump constructed under this paragraph
as they have in relation to a road hump constructed by them under
paragraph 4.

(5) Where a road hump has been constructed under this paragraph,
the local highway authority may reimburse the Secretary of State
the whole or part of his expenses in relation to the road hump.

Consultation and local inquiries

6.—(1) Where the Secretary of State or a local highway authority
propose to construct a road hump under paragraph 4 or 5, he or
they shall consult with—

    (*a*) the chief officer of police for the area in which the highway
        concerned is situated ; and

    (*b*) such other persons or bodies as may be prescribed by regula-
        tions made by the Secretary of State.

(2) The Secretary of State or local highway authority shall also—

    (*a*) publish in one or more newspapers circulating in the area
        in which the highway concerned is situated ; and

    (*b*) place at appropriate points on that highway,

a notice of the proposal stating the nature, dimensions and location
of the proposed road hump and the address to which and the period
within which any objections to the proposal may be sent.

(3) The period stated in a notice under sub-paragraph (2) shall
be not less than 21 days beginning with the date on which the
notice is first published in accordance with paragraph (*a*) of that
sub-paragraph.

(4) The Secretary of State or local highway authority shall consider
any objection sent to him or them in accordance with a notice
under sub-paragraph (2) and may, if he or they think fit, cause a
local inquiry to be held.

(5) Subsections (2) to (8) of section 210 of the Local Government 1973 c. 65.
(Scotland) Act 1973 (provisions as to inquiries) have effect in relation
to an inquiry held under sub-paragraph (4) as they have effect in

relation to an inquiry held under that section, but with such modifications as may be prescribed by regulations made by the Secretary of State.

(6) Before making regulations under this paragraph the Secretary of State shall consult such representative organisations as he thinks fit.

Regulations concerning construction and maintenance of road humps

7.—(1) The Secretary of State may by regulations make such provision in relation to the construction and maintenance of road humps as appears to him to be necessary or expedient in the interests of safety and the free movement of traffic, and may in particular—

(a) provide that road humps shall be constructed only on highways of such descriptions and in such circumstances as may be prescribed by the regulations ;

(b) impose requirements as to—

(i) the nature, dimensions, location and spacing of road humps ;

(ii) the placing of signs of such type or character as may be so prescribed ;

(iii) the carrying out and maintenance of other ancillary or consequential works.

(2) Regulations under this paragraph may make different provision for different cases, as for example for road humps and highways of different descriptions.

(3) Before making any regulations under this paragraph the Secretary of State shall consult with such representative organisations as he thinks fit.

(4) Regulations under this paragraph do not apply where a road hump is specially authorised by the Secretary of State, but conditions attached by him to the authorisation may, in particular, relate to any of the matters with respect to which regulations may be made under this paragraph.

(5) In this paragraph and in paragraph 8 and 9(1) below, and without prejudice to paragraph 9(2) below, the expression " highway " includes any road over which the public have a right of way.

Status of road humps

8.—(1) Where a road hump conforms to regulations under paragraph 7 and, in the case of a road hump constructed under paragraph 4 or 5 above, the condition mentioned in sub-paragraph (2) is satisfied, the road hump shall not be treated as constituting on obstruction to the highway but as part of the highway, so that in particular—

(a) the obligation of any person to maintain the highway ; and

(b) the obligation of any person having power to break open the highway to make good any damage or otherwise reinstate the highway ;

extend to maintaining or, as the case may be, to making good any damage to or otherwise reinstating the road hump.

(2) The further condition applicable in the case of a road hump   Sch. 10
constructed under paragraph 4 or 5 above is that either—

  (*a*) the highway in question is for the time being subject to a
        statutory speed limit for motor vehicles of 30 miles per
        hour or less : or

  (*b*) the road hump is specially authorised by the Secretary of
        State.

(3) In relation to a road hump specially authorised by the Secretary of State the reference in sub-paragraph (1) to conformity with regulations shall be construed as a reference to conformity with the conditions attached to the authorisation.

(4) In so far as it does not apply apart from this sub-paragraph, Part II of the Public Utilities Street Works Act 1950 (code regulating   1950 c. 39. relations between persons carrying out alterations to roads and statutory undertakers having apparatus in those roads) applies in relation to the construction, maintenance and removal of a road hump as if the works were executed for road purposes and were mentioned in section 21(1)(*a*) of that Act and as if the person executing them were the promoting authority within the meaning of that Part.

Interpretation and construction

9.—(1) In this Part—

  " motor vehicle " has the same meaning as in the Road Traffic   1967 c. 76.
        Regulation Act 1967 ;

  " road hump " means an artificial hump in or on the surface of
        the highway which is designed to control the speed of
        vehicles, and references to a road hump include references
        to any other works (including signs or lighting) required in
        connection with such a hump ;

  " statutory " means having effect by virtue of an enactment.

(2) This Part shall be construed as one with the Roads (Scotland)   1970 c. 20. Act 1970.

SCHEDULE 11   Section 33.

Factors Determining Rates of Vehicle Excise Duty in respect of Goods Vehicles

Part I

Main Factors

Table 1

*Goods vehicles of a gross or train weight
not exceeding 12 metric tonnes*

Description of vehicle	Factors determining rate of duty
Rigid goods vehicle not drawing trailer or drawing unladen trailer.	Gross weight of vehicle.
Rigid goods vehicle drawing laden trailer.	Gross weight of vehicle and gross weight of trailer.
Articulated goods vehicle.	Train weight of vehicle.

TABLE 2
*Goods vehicles of gross or train weight
exceeding* 12 *metric tonnes*

Description of vehicle	Factors determining rate of duty
Rigid goods vehicle not drawing trailer or drawing unladen trailer.	Gross weight of vehicle and number of axles on vehicle.
Rigid goods vehicle drawing laden trailer.	Gross weight of vehicle, gross weight of trailer and number of axles on vehicle.
Articulated goods vehicle.	Train weight of vehicle, number of axles on drawing vehicle and minimum number of axles on drawn vehicle.

PART II

ADDITIONAL FACTORS

1. The equality or disparity of the weight transmitted through each of the two rear-most axles of the vehicle (or, if it is an articulated vehicle, of the drawing vehicle).

2. The number of axles on the laden trailer drawn by a rigid goods vehicle.

Section 40.

SCHEDULE 12

REPEALS

PART I

REPEALS CONSEQUENTIAL ON PART II

Chapter	Short title	Extent of repeal
1962 c. 46.	Transport Act 1962.	Section 1(5). Section 9. Section 19(3)(iii). In Schedule 9— (*a*) paragraph 1; (*b*) the lists in paragraphs 2(1) and 3(1) of the harbours vesting in the Docks Board.
1964 c. 40.	Harbours Act 1964.	In section 30(1)(*b*), the words " the British Transport Docks Board ". In section 36(*a*), the words " the British Transport Docks Board ". In section 57(1), in the definition of " the Boards ", the words " the British Transport Docks Board,".

SCH. 12

Chapter	Short title	Extent of repeal
1968 c. 73.	Transport Act 1968.	Section 41(7). In section 50(1), the words " Docks Board ". In Schedule 16, in paragraph 8(2), the words " the Docks Board ".
1975 c. 24.	House of Commons Disqualification Act 1975.	In Part II of Schedule 1, the entry for the British Transport Docks Board.
1975 c. 25.	Northern Ireland Assembly Disqualification Act 1975.	In Part II of Schedule 1, the entry for the British Transport Docks Board.
1980 c. 66.	Highways Act 1980.	In section 219(4)(*i*)(i), the words " the British Transport Docks Board ".

PART II

REPEALS CONSEQUENTIAL ON PART III

Chapter	Short Title	Extent of Repeal
1964 c. 40.	Harbours Act 1964.	Sections 1 to 8. Section 9(6). In section 11(1), the words " and after consulting the Council ". Section 12. Section 14(6). In section 15, in subsection (1) the words " on a representation made to him by the Council ", and subsection (2). Section 16(8). In section 17(1), paragraphs (*c*) to (*f*), (*h*) and (*i*). In section 18(1), the words " by the Council or ". Sections 20 to 25. In section 31(2), the words from the first " and " to " sections ". In section 31(13), the words from " and in relation " to the end. Sections 32 to 34, both as originally enacted and as applied by any enactment. In section 35, the words " 32 and 34 ", the words from " and of securing " to " with the like consequences) ", and the paragraphs from (*h*) onwards.

Chapter	Short Title	Extent of Repeal
1964 c. 40—*cont.*	Harbours Act 1964—*cont.*	In section 36, the words " and 32 ". In section 37, the words " to 33 ". Section 41(2). In section 43— (*a*) in subsection (1), the words " 6 or "; (*b*) in subsection (2), the words " 6 or ". In section 44— (*a*) in subsection (1), the words from " or who desires " to " parcel of land " and the words from " under the said Act of 1945 " to " it is made) "; (*b*) in subsection (1A), the words " relating to a harbour revision or empowerment order "; (*c*) subsection (2); (*d*) in subsection (3), the words from " and an order " to the end; (*e*) in subsection (5), the words " and (2)(*a*) ". In section 45(*a*), the words " 4 or ". In section 46(1)— (*a*) the words " 4 or "; (*b*) in paragraph (*c*) the words " the Council or " and " their or ". In section 47(1)— (*a*) paragraph (*a*)(i); (*b*) the word " and " at the end of paragraph (*a*); (*c*) paragraph (*b*); (*d*) the words " (i) and ". In section 47(2) the words from " and shall " to " Act " where next occurring, and paragraph (*a*). In section 49(2) the words " and an order under section 20 of this Act ". In section 54(2), the words " 4,", " 20," and " 23 ". In section 57(1), the definitions of " accounting period ", " control of movement order " and " the Council ". In section 62(1), the words " or an order under section 20 of this Act ".

Chapter	Short Title	Extent of Repeal
1964 c. 40—*cont.*	Harbours Act 1964—*cont.*	Schedule 1. In Schedule 3— (*a*) paragraph 2; (*b*) in paragraph 4 and in paragraph 8, sub-paragraph (2) and sub-paragraph (3) from " and after " onwards; (*c*) in the heading to Part I, the words from " TO THE MINISTER OF AGRICULTURE " to " PART IV) " and the words from " BY THE MINISTER OF AGRICULTURE " to the end; (*d*) in the heading to Part II, the words from " (AS SET OUT) " to the end; (*e*) Parts III to VI, VIII and IX. In Schedule 4— (*a*) paragraph 2(*c*); (*b*) in paragraph 2(*d*) the words from " if " to " Council "; (*c*) paragraph 3(2), (3) and (4); (*d*) in paragraph 3(5) the words " the scheme was submitted otherwise than by the Council and " and the words from " and after " onwards; (*e*) in paragraph 4 the words " (*c*) or " and the words from " according " onwards. Schedule 5.
1966 c. 28.	Docks and Harbours Act 1966.	In section 6— (*a*) in subsection (1) the words " the Council "; (*b*) in subsection (3) the words " the Council and ". In section 7— (*a*) in subsection (2) the words " and the Council "; (*b*) subsections (3) to (5); (*c*) in subsection (6) the words " or making an objection or representations "; (*d*) in subsection (7) the words from " or a copy " to " such appeal " and the words " objection or representations ";

Chapter	Short Title	Extent of Repeal
1966 c. 28— *cont.*	Docks and Harbours Act 1966—*cont.*	(*e*) in subsection (8) the words from " or a copy " to " such an appeal " and the words " objection or representations "; (*f*) subsection (9); (*g*) in subsection (10) the words " or an objection is made thereunder to " and the words " or objection to " in both places; (*h*) subsection (11); (*i*) subsection (12) except paragraph (*c*), and in that paragraph the words from the first " and " to " subsection " and the final " and ". In section 8— (*a*) in subsection (1) the words " or an objection is made thereunder to "; (*b*) in subsection (2) the words " or objection ", in both places, the words " or objected to " and the words " or the objection is made to "; (*c*) in subsections (3) and (5) the words " or an objection made to "; (*d*) in subsection (4) the words " or objection to "; (*e*) in subsection (6) the words " or objection " and the words " the Council ". In section 9— (*a*) in subsection (2) the words " or objecting to ", " or an objection is made to ", " or objection " and " or objections to "; (*b*) in subsection (3) the words " the Council and "; (*c*) in subsection (4) the words " or an objection made to " and the words " or objection " in both places; (*d*) in subsection (5) the words " or objection ". In section 10(3)— (*a*) in paragraph (*b*), the words " or objecting to ", " or an objection is made to " and " or objection ";

Chapter	Short Title	Extent of Repeal
1966 c. 28—*cont.*	Docks and Harbours Act 1966—*cont.*	(*b*) in paragraph (*c*), the words " or an objection is made to " and " or objection ". In section 11— (*a*) in subsection (4) the words " the Council "; (*b*) in subsection (5) the words " or an objection made to " and " or objection "; (*c*) in subsection (8) the words " the Council ", and in paragraph (*b*) the words from " (if " to " thereto) "; (*d*) in subsection (9) the words from " and the Council " to " that decision " and the words " or objection ", in both places; (*e*) in subsection (10) the words from " and if an objection " onwards. In section 12(3) the words " the Council ". In section 15(1)— (*a*) in paragraph (*b*), the words " or objection to ", " or objection " and " or objecting "; (*b*) in paragraph (*c*), the words " or objection " in both places. Section 40(1) to (4). In section 42(2)(*a*) the words " (3) or ", where first occurring, and the words from " the said " onwards. Section 44(4). Sections 48 and 49. In section 52(2)(*a*), the words " or objection ". In section 58, in subsection (1) the definition of " the Council ", and in subsection (5) the words " or an objection is made " and the words " or objection ".
1967 c. 80.	Criminal Justice Act 1967.	In Schedule 3, in Part II the amendment of the Harbours Act 1964.
1968 c. 13.	National Loans Act 1968.	In Schedule 1, the entry for section 6(1)(*b*) of the Harbours Act 1964.
1969 c. 48.	Post Office Act 1969.	In Schedule 4, in paragraph 93, in sub-paragraphs (1)(xxii) and (2)(*k*), the words " and 5 ". In Schedule 5, in paragraph 5(*t*), the words " and 5 ".

SCH. 12

Chapter	Short title	Extent of repeal
1971 c. 75.	Civil Aviation Act 1971.	In Schedule 4, the entry relating to the National Ports Council.
1972 c. 11.	Superannuation Act 1972.	In Schedule 6, paragraph 45.
1972 c. 16.	Harbours (Loans) Act 1972.	In section 1(1), the words " after consulting the National Ports Council ". In section 1(4), the words " 6 or ".
1975 c. 24.	House of Commons Dis-qualification Act 1975.	In Part II of Schedule 1, the entry for the National Ports Council.
1976 c. 79.	Dock Work Regulation Act 1976.	In section 2(5), the words " with the National Ports Council and ". In section 7(8), paragraph (*a*). In section 8(6), paragraph (*a*).

PART III

REPEALS CONSEQUENTIAL ON PARTS IV AND V

Chapter	Short title	Extent of repeal
10 & 11 Vict. c. 89.	The Town Police Clauses Act 1847.	Section 39.
33 & 34 Vict. c. 115.	The Metropolitan Public Carriage Act 1869.	In section 6 the words " at such price ". In section 8 the words " at such price ".
1923 c. 27.	The Railway Fires Act (1905) Amendment Act 1923.	Section 1. In section 2, the words " not exceeding the said sum of two hundred pounds ".
1972 c. 20.	The Road Traffic Act 1972.	In section 89, in subsection (1), in paragraph (*aa*) the words " or (*c*) ", and paragraph (*c*) and the word " and " preceding it. In section 90, in subsection (1), paragraph (*bb*). In section 93, subsections (3) and (5). In section 177(2)(*c*) the words from " (whether or not " to " section 93(3) of this Act) ". In section 189, in subsection (1), paragraph (*g*). In Schedule 4, in Part V, paragraph 1.
1974 c. 50.	The Road Traffic Act 1974.	Section 17. In Schedule 3, in the paragraphs set out in paragraph 6, paragraph (*bb*).

Chapter	Short title	Extent of repeal
1975 c. xxix.	The British Railways (No. 2) Act 1975.	Section 21.
1977 c. xii.	The London Transport Act 1977.	Section 13(1).
1977 c. xvii.	The British Railways Act 1977.	Section 14(1).
1980 c. 62.	The Criminal Justice (Scotland) Act 1980.	In Schedule 7, paragraph 22.
1981 c. 14.	The Public Passenger Vehicles Act 1981.	In Schedule 7, paragraph 24. In Schedule 8, in the entry relating to the Transport Act 1968, the words " In section 145, subsection (2) ".

PRINTED IN ENGLAND BY W. J. SHARP
Controller and Chief Executive of Her Majesty's Stationery Office and
Queen's Printer of Acts of Parliament